AT PEACE W

CIVIL WAR BURIALS OF LAUREL HILL CEMETERY
PHILADELPHIA, PENNSYLVANIA

Compiled & Edited
by
Blake A. Magner

Collingswood
C. W. HISTORICALS
1997

Copyright© 1997 by Blake A. Magner

All rights reserved. No part of this publication may be used or reproduced without written permission of the publisher, except in the case of brief quotations used in reviews or essays.

ISBN 0-9637745-2-2

Printed in the United States of America

First Edition

Front Cover: GRAVE OF ROBERT PATTERSON
Laurel Hill Cemetery

Back Cover: THE FUNERAL OF GEN. GEORGE GORDON MEADE
Laurel Hill Cemetery, Philadelphia, Pennsylvania, November 11, 1872.

C.W. Historicals
PO Box 113
Collingswood, N.J. 08108

Dedicated to the memory
of
John Francis Marion

Laurel Hill Cemetery
3822 Ridge Avenue
Philadelphia, Pennsylvania 19132
215-228-8200

Hours: Tuesday - Saturday: 9:30 a.m. to 1.30 p.m.
Closed Sunday, Monday, and holidays

Introduction

As John Francis Marion, Philadelphia historian, author, and (not least) tour guide often pointed out, Laurel Hill Cemetery is a museum of Philadelphia history. There is nothing accidental about this. It was conceived from the beginning as a place that would straddle the line between public and private.

Laurel Hill is a distinctively Victorian cemetery. When the nation was born, Americans were buried either in the churchyard or in a small plot on the family farm. By the 1830s, however, the churchyard was becoming overcrowded and some enterprising real estate man wanted to buy the farm, move the bodies, and build a town.

In 1836, Laurel Hill offered a new possibility. It was designed by architect John Notman as a rolling landscape overlooking the Schuylkill River. Each family could have its own plot in perpetuity, protected by an ornate cast-iron fence amid beautiful shrubs and flowers.

There were no public parks when Laurel Hill was founded. Philadelphians who wanted to enjoy a pleasant stroll in a picturesque surrounding came to Laurel Hill. Thousands came on Sunday afternoons, so many that the cemetery company began issuing tickets in an effort to control the crowds. Each monument would be seen by a huge number of people. If there was a place to proclaim family accomplishments, this was it. Statues that would now go straight to Fairmount Park were then erected in Laurel Hill.

A visitor strolling through Laurel Hill examining the amazing number of Civil War graves that Blake Magner has identified will see that families combined the public and private in many different ways. General George Gordon Meade's monument is meant for the family. It says nothing about the battle of Gettysburg. General Robert Patterson's monument, by contrast, is addressed to the public. It gives the dates of the three ways in which he served and is topped by a life-size lion symbolizing his military courage.

Most families combined the public and private. They gave the intimate details that the family would want, but also, at least some of the details of military service. They wanted the military careers of their husbands and fathers to be remembered.

Laurel Hill Cemetery lost some of its public character in the Twentieth Century. With less money coming in from families, maintenance suffered. A visitor to Laurel Hill thirty years ago stepped into a part of the city that had been almost entirely forgotten.

Fortunately, John Francis Marion, to whom Blake Magner has dedicated this book, was such a visitor. Born in Norfolk, Virginia, raised in Rochester, New York, and educated at Penn State, John was one of the most enthusiastic people who ever made Philadelphia his adopted home. He at once saw that Laurel Hill Cemetery was a much too important cultural monument to be neglected. He wrote about it in his book *Famous and Curious Cemeteries* and he began leading tours.

Working with Jane and Drayton Smith, he founded The Friends of Laurel Hill Cemetery to raise funds for the preservation of the cemetery's landscape and its monuments. The cemetery will never again attract thousands on a Sunday afternoon but the Friends' tours now attract well over a thousand each year. And visitors with *At Peace With Honor* in hand will have a direct pathway to a vital period in America's history.

Michael Brooks
The Friends of Laurel Hill Cemetery
Wayne, Pennsylvania
September 1995

Preface and Acknowledgments

I have always been drawn to cemeteries in one way or another, not through a morbid curiosity, but rather from a sense of kinship with those who have gone before. Growing up in the small Massachusetts town of Warwick, where there were more than twice as many residents in the local cemetery than were living in the village, I was able roam the grounds seeing 200 years of the town's history. Added to this there were the numerous family plots scattered throughout the area, most overgrown by vegetation and abandoned, that contained perhaps only a few markers. These small burial grounds peeked the imagination, making one wonder who the occupants were and what had happened that led the plots to be abandoned and forgotten. It was only natural that my interest would grow as an adult.

I first became familiar with Laurel Hill Cemetery in 1990, shortly before the 175th anniversary of the birth of General George Gordon Meade. Since then I have been on numerous tours of the cemetery, even leading a few myself. With more than thirty-five years of interest in the American Civil War, it was inevitable that I would seek out the burials that pertained to those tragic years, 1861-1865. Through my research, and numerous hours of trudging around the Cemetery grounds, I managed to more than double the list of generals and period notables known to be interred on the grounds. Some of these personalities were the most prominent of the war.

Philadelphia, rich in Civil War history, has more than 175 Civil War generals buried within a fifty mile radius. Laurel Hill, with thirty-one generals and a number of naval officers, ranks about fifth in the nation for such interments. The Cemetery also has hundreds of other burials related to the war, some of which are presented here.

There are many people I have to thank for their assistance in putting this book together. First there is Roger Hunt of Rockville, Maryland, for sharing his wealth of knowledge on the brevet brigadier generals, and a couple of colonels, as well as his photographic collection. Then there are the contributors, who put their time into producing this volume. At Laurel Hill there is Michael Brooks for his introduction, John Fitale, the Cemetery superintendent, and Joe Direso, the general manager, for their wandering around the cemetery with me in order to find the unmarked plots and for digging through the files looking for information. I also thank Barney McAllister, for letting me in the Cemetery doors on my numerous visits, Marie Kalinoski for her help, and Barbara K. Smith, President of the Friends of Laurel Hill Cemetery. My thanks also goes to Mr. Richard Wood Snowdon, Jr., a descendent of the Pattersons, for graciously allowing me to use the photograph of the Patterson plot on the front cover. To Gerard White of the Congressional Medal of Honor Society, thank you. There is Mary Hush for her assistance in editing this volume, Linda Duffy who came through with needed material that unfortunately I did not use, Michael Winey for a great last minute tip on GATH, and Mike Cavanaugh for an even later tip on symbolism in the Cemetery. Lastly there is Rosa and Stewart B. Harkness, Jr., without whose research no one would be able to write about Laurel Hill Cemetery. And for those whom I have failed to mention and deserve it, thank you.

I also wish to thank my wife Johanna and son Bradley for allowing me the hours at Laurel Hill and the even longer hours in front of the computer.

Blake A. Magner
Westmont, New Jersey
May 1997

Contributors

(BAM) Blake A. Magner makes his living as a Civil War historian, publisher, photographer, cartographer, and author. He holds a Masters Degree in Biology from Rutgers University and has chosen to pursue his passion of the Civil War as apposed to his formal education. He has had his work published in more than sixty books and publications including *Civil War Times Illustrated*, *Military Images*, and *Gettysburg Magazine*. Magner is co-author of *Battlefield Commanders: Gettysburg,* and is author of *Traveller & Company: The Horses of Gettysburg.*

(MB) Michael Brooks received his Ph. D. from the University of Toronto and is a professor of English Literature at West Chester University. He is the author of *John Ruskins Victorian Architecture*, a member of the Board of Directors of Laurel Hill Cemetery, and the chief cemetery tour guide.

(TEB) Terry Buckalew lives in Wyndmoor, Pennsylvania, with his wife Marilyn and their two children. He has managed historical properties for the University of Pennsylvania since 1982. He invites any inquiries or information concerning Benny Hodgson.

(DH) David Hann is a member of numerous Civil War groups, including the Sons of Union Veterans in which he is a New Jersey Department Commander, and the Sons of Confederate Veterans. He is a reenactor with Co. A, 148th Pennsylvania, and is also a descendent of Colonel Charles Ellet of whom he writes in this volume.

(PEP) Patrick E. Purcell is a retired Consolidated Rail Corporation manager. A graduate of Northeastern University, he was a sergeant in the Army Transportation Corps. He is managing editor of the National Railway Historical Society magazine, a certified member of the American Society of Transportation and Logistics, and is presently the president of the Civil War Round Table of Philadelphia.

(THS) Timothy H. Smith is a life long student of the battle of Gettysburg and an authority on the First Day's fighting. He is a volunteer at the Adams County Historical Society and a Board Member of the Gettysburg Battlefield Preservation Association. He has written articles for various Civil War publications and is the author of a book entitled, *The Story of Lee's Headquarters, Gettysburg, Pennsylvania.* He is currently employed as a Licensed Battlefield Guide at the Gettysburg National Military Park.

(SJW) Steven J. Wright is the curator of collections at the Civil War Library and Museum in Philadelphia, Pennsylvania. He holds history degrees from St John's University (Minnesota) and the University of Minnesota-Duluth. He is the author of *The Irish Brigade*, as well as various magazine articles on the Civil War and is also a book reviewer for *The Civil War News* and *The Courier.*

Henry Harrison Bingham was born in Philadelphia, Pennsylvania, on December 4, 1841. After graduating college (Jefferson College in Canonsburg, Pennsylvania) he entered the 140th Pennsylvania Volunteers on August 22, 1862. By September he had attained the rank of captain.

During the battle of Gettysburg, Bingham was serving on the staff of Major General Winfield Scott Hancock. At the culmination of the battle, during the Pickett-Pettigrew Assault, Confederate General Lewis Armistead (an old pre-war Regular Army friend of Hancock) was wounded after he crossed the stone wall near the famous Copse of Trees. Calling out in such a way as to identify himself as a Mason, a number of Federals came to Armistead's assistance, one of whom stole his sword.

As Armistead was being carried off the field by a group of privates, they came upon Captain Bingham, a fellow Mason, who identified himself and told Armistead that if he had anything of value that he would take care of it. Armistead asked for General Hancock and instructed Bingham, "Tell Gen. Hancock for me that I have done him and done you all an injury which I shall regret or repent (Bingham did not remember the exact word) the longest day I live." At this time the Captain took Armistead's spurs, watch, chain, seal, and pocketbook, which were later delivered to Hancock.

Bingham was promoted to major and Judge Advocate on September 20, 1864, and continued to serve on Hancock's staff. He was breveted brigadier general, USV, on April 9, 1865, "for conspicuous gallantry and meritorious services during the war." He was mustered out of the service on July 2, 1866.

Bingham was appointed postmaster of Philadelphia in March 1867, resigning in December 1872. He then accepted the clerkship of the Quarter Sessions Court, to which he was reelected in 1875. Bingham served as a delegate from the First Congressional District in the Republican National Convention in Cincinnati (1876), Chicago (1884 & 1888), Minneapolis (1892), St. Louis (1896), and Philadelphia (1900). Elected to Congress in 1879, Bingham served there until his death. During that time Bingham received the distinction of becoming "the Father of the House," for not only being the senior member, but having served longer than any man in the history of the House, thirty-three years, nineteen days.

On August 26, 1893, Bingham was awarded the Medal of Honor for his actions at the battle of The Wilderness, where he "rallied under fire a body of badly demoralized troops and led them in a successful charge against the enemy." Bingham died in Philadelphia on March 22, 1912.

Today, in the annex adjoining the

Soldiers' National Cemetery in Gettysburg, stands the Friend to Friend Masonic Monument. Dedicated on August 21, 1993, the sculpture captures the moment that Bingham met and consoled the wounded Armistead. (BAM)

Sources:
Ladd, David L., and Audry J. Ladd. Bingham to Hancock, January 5, 1869. *The Bachelder Papers: Gettysburg in Their Own Words*. Volume I. Dayton. 1994.
Laurel Hill Cemetery, Burial records, H. H. Bingham. Philadelphia, Pennsylvania.
Magner, Blake A. (ed.). *The Gettysburg Encyclopedia*. Unpublished manuscript.
USGPO, *The Medal of Honor of the United States Army*. Washington. 1948.

Cemetery Location: Section Y, Lots 105 & 107.

Inscription:
    Gen. H. H. Bingham
    1841-1912
    Post No. 1, G.A.R. Penna
    At Rest

Bronze Plaque:
    Henry H. Bingham
    Medal of Honor
    Brig. Gen. US Vols
    Civil War
    Dec 4 1841 Mar 22 1912

George Alexander Hamilton Blake was born on August 31, 1810, in Philadelphia. Spending his life in the Regular Army, he began his career as a lieutenant in the 2nd Dragoons on June 11, 1836. Promoted to captain in December 1839, Blake participated in the Seminole Wars, taking part in the 1841 actions at Fort Miller and Jupiter Inlet. During his service in the Mexican War he participated in the battles of Cerro Gordo, Puebla, Contreras, Molino del Rey, Chapultepec, and Mexico City. For gallant conduct at St. Augustine, Blake was brevetted a major. He was promoted to major of the 1st Dragoons

March 13, 1865, he was brevetted brigadier general for his services at Gettysburg.

Blake was a member of a military commission in Washington during 1865 and 1866, and then commanded Fort Vancouver in Washington Territory. He retired on December 15, 1870, and died in Washington, D.C., on October 27, 1884. (BAM)

Cemetery Location: Section H, Lot 68.

Inscription:
His tender mercies are over all his works
Gen'l George A. H. Blake
1st Cavalry USA
Born Aug. 31, 1810
Died October 27, 1884

Sources:
Appleton's Cyclopedia of American Biography (7 vols.). New York. 1898.
Hunt, Roger D., and Jack R. Brown. *Brevet Brigadier Generals in Blue*. Gaithersburg. 1990.

and served on the frontier against the Apache and Navajo Indians.

In May 1861, Blake became the lieutenant colonel of the 1st U.S. Cavalry and on December 15, 1862, the colonel. He was slightly wounded at Gaines's Mill and participated in the actions at Aldie, Middleburg, Upperville, and Gettysburg, where he distinguished himself. During this time he served as the Chief Commissary of Musters in the Department of Virginia and as part of the Cavalry Corps of the Army of the Potomac. He remained on special duty with the Cavalry Bureau until the end of the war. On

William Henry Charles Bohlen was born in Bremen, Germany, on October 22, 1810. He came to the United States when he was a young man and settled in Philadelphia, where he amassed a considerable fortune as a liquor merchant.

Having possibly served in the Mexican War, at the outbreak of the Civil War Bohlen was instrumental in raising the 75th Pennsylvania Infantry, a largely German regiment. Bohlen was appointed regimental colonel on September 30, 1861. After serving near Washington, Bohlen's command was transferred to the command

Bohlen's body was returned to Philadelphia, where it was placed in the family vault in front of St. John's Evangelical Lutheran Church on Race Street below Sixth. When the Benjamin Franklin Bridge was built connecting Camden, New Jersey, and Philadelphia, thus closing the church's burial ground, the Bohlen family remains were moved to Laurel Hill Cemetery. (BAM)

of General Louis Blenker and sent to the mountain Department under General John C. Frémont. On April 28, 1862, Bohlen was promoted to brigadier general, U.S. Volunteers.

During Confederate General Thomas "Stonewall" Jackson's 1862 Valley Campaign, Bohlen distinguished himself at the battle of Cross Keys. Later, as part of the Army of Virginia, Bohlen's command covered the retreat of various army units after the battle of Cedar Mountain. On August 22, 1862, Bohlen's Brigade took part in an action against Jackson's Confederates at Freeman's Ford, just above Rappahannock Station, Virginia. Bohlen was killed while attempting to get his command back across the Rappahannock River.

Cemetery Location: Section Y, Lot 34.

Inscription:
Brigadier General W. Henry C. Bohlen
U.S. Volunteers
Born on the 22nd day of October 1810
Killed in action at
Freeman's Ford Rappahannock River, Virginia
on the 22nd day of August 1862.

Sources:
Appleton's Cyclopedia of American Biography (7 vols.). New York. 1898.
Bates, Samuel P. *History of Pennsylvania Volunteers* (5 vols.). Harrisburg. 1869.

Warner, Ezra. *Generals in Blue: Lives of the Union Commanders*. Baton Rouge. 1864.

Gideon Clark was born in Philadelphia on June 19, 1822. After receiving an academic education he was apprenticed to the engraving business. After his apprenticeship, he began his own business in which he gained a reputation as being a skillful and conscientious workman. Coming from a military family, Clark joined the militia as part of the Philadelphia Grays which participated in the city riots of 1844.

At the outbreak of the Civil War, Clark was a second lieutenant in the Grays and volunteered for Lincoln's first call for troops. He was appointed adjutant of the 17th Pennsylvania Volunteers under the command of fellow Philadelphian Frank E. Patterson. The regiment was mustered out of service on August 2, 1861, and Clark was then commissioned lieutenant colonel of the 119th Pennsylvania. This regiment participated in many of the battles of the Army of the Potomac. At the action near Rappahannock Station, Virginia, Clark commanded the regiment. He later distinguished himself for bravery at the battle of Salem Heights.

In January 1864, Clark was placed in permanent command of the regiment taking part in the battle of The Wilderness. In June, he commanded the brigade and was praised for good conduct at the battle of Cold Harbor. On March 13, 1865, he was breveted colonel and brigadier general "for gallant and meritorious conduct and services performed in 1865 in storming the works of the enemy in front of Petersburg, Virginia." On March 25, he was slightly wounded in the fighting around Petersburg. Clark was again seriously wounded on April 2, and spent the remainder of the war in the hospital.

After the war, Clark returned to Philadelphia where he changed from the Democrat to the Republican party and became a school director. In October 1866, he was appointed Master Warden of the Port of Philadelphia where he served for six years. He later became a bank assessor and then collector of delinquent taxes. In 1873, Clark was elected to the office of Register of Wills and in the early 1880s served two terms in the Common Council.

Clark was a member of the Philadelphia Commandery NO. 2, Knight Templars of Post 2, G.A.R., and a member of the Volunteer Fire Association. General Clark died in Philadelphia on May 24, 1897. (BAM)

Cemetery Location: Section 8, Lot 51.

Inscription:
> FATHER
> Gen. Gideon Clark
> Born June 19, 1822
> Died May 24, 1897
> Last Call
>
> CLARK

Sources:
Bates, Samuel P. *Martial Deeds of Pennsylvania*. Philadelphia. 1875.
Clark File. Cemetery Records. Laurel Hill Cemetery. Philadelphia, PA.
Hunt, Roger D., and Jack R. Brown. *Brevet Brigadier Generals in Blue*. Gaithersburg. 1990.

Thomas Jefferson Cram was born in Unity, New Hampshire, in March 1804. He graduated from the United States Military Academy in 1826, fourth in a class of forty-one. He served at the Academy as an assistant professor of mathematics from 1826 to 1829, and of natural and experimental philosophy from 1829 to 1836. Resigning on September 16, 1836, for the next two years Cram acted as an assistant engineer on railroads in Maryland and Pennsylvania. He rejoined the Regular Army as a captain on July 7, 1838, and served as a topographical engineer. He aided in reconnaissances in Texas, and from 1855 to 1859 served as the Chief Topographical Engineer in the Department of the Pacific.

Cram was promoted to major on August 6, 1861, then lieutenant colonel that September. On March 3, 1863, he transferred to the engineer corps. During this period he acted as an aide-de-camp to Major General John E. Wool, where he participated in the capture of Norfolk, Virginia. Promoted to colonel in November 1865, he was again promoted, this time to brigadier general and then major general on January 13, 1865, for his services during the war.

After the Civil War, Cram served on a number of boards of engineers which improved harbors along the Great Lakes. He retired in February 22, 1869, and died in Philadelphia on December 20, 1883. (BAM)

Cemetery Location: Section 3, Lot 106.

Inscription:
> T. J. Cram
> Dec. 20, 1883

Sources:
Appleton's Cyclopedia of American Biography (7 vols.). New York. 1898.

Hunt, Roger D., and Jack R. Brown. *Brevet Brigadier Generals in Blue*. Gaithersburg. 1990.

Samuel Wylie Crawford was born in Franklin County, Pennsylvania, on November 8, 1829. He graduated from the University of Pennsylvania in 1846, and then the University's medical school in 1850. The following year he joined the army and accepted an appointment as an assistant surgeon, serving on the Western Frontier until 1861. Transferred to Fort Moultrie in Charleston, South Carolina, Crawford was in command of a battery during the bombardment of Fort Sumter on April 12, 1861.

Crawford resigned his staff position and on May 14 was commissioned major of the newly created 13th U.S. Infantry. On April 25, 1862, he was promoted to brigadier general and placed in command of the First Brigade, First Division, of Banks's Fifth Corps taking part in the battle of Winchester. At the battle of

Cedar Mountain, as part of the Second Corps, Army of Virginia, Crawford's brigade suffered fifty percent casualties. Then, as part of the Twelfth Corps at Antietam, he succeeded to Division command before being severely wounded.

In May 1863, Crawford was assigned to the command of the Pennsylvania Reserves. He led his division with distinction at Gettysburg as part of Sykes's Fifth Corps. His men were heavily engaged during Longstreet's attack on July 2. Later taking part in the 1864 Overland Campaign and the siege of Petersburg, Crawford was breveted for gallantry for his actions at The Wilderness, Spotsylvania, Jericho Mills, Bethesda Church, Five Forks, and Petersburg. He was breveted through all grades to major general in the Volunteer and Regular Armies.

Crawford was mustered out of volunteer service in 1866. Returning to the Regular Army, he served at various posts in the South, gaining promotion to colonel in 1869. Crawford retired on February 19, 1873, and in 1875 he was promoted to brigadier general on the retired list. Moving to Philadelphia, General Crawford lived there until his death on November 3, 1892. (BAM)

Cemetery Location: Section L, Lot 69.

Inscription:

FORT SUMTER   GETTYSBURG
Brev. Maj. Gen. S. W. Crawford   USA
Born   November 8, 1827
Died   November 3, 1892
CRAWFORD

Sources:
Appleton's Cyclopedia of American Biography (7 vols.). New York. 1898.
Warner, Ezra. *Generals in Blue: Lives of the Union Commanders*. Baton Rouge. 1864.

Alexander Cummings was born on November 17, 1810, in Williamsport, Pennsylvania. He became a printer and later entered the newspaper business in Philadelphia. In 1845 he bought a one half interest in the Philadelphia *North American* which he sold two years later. In April 1847, he published the first issue of *Cummings' Evening Telegraphic Bulletin* which, ten years later, became the Philadelphia *Evening Bulletin*. He remained the publisher of the *Bulletin* until 1859, and in 1860 founded the New York *World*. The *World* was a semi-religious paper which did not fare well. By late 1862, it was controlled by men, other than Cummings, who dropped the religious slant and changed its politics from Republican to Democrat.

At the outbreak of the Civil War, Cummings was appointed a special purchasing agent for the War Department by Secretary of War Simon Cameron. It was his responsibility to expedite the defense of Washington, D.C., by making arrangements with the railroads for troop transportation. He was also responsible for the purchase of needed supplies and equipment. He was a dismal failure, at one point buying 20,000 straw hats and 19,680 pairs of linen pants which were subsequently ruled "out of uniform" by the military. He was never able to live down the nickname he received from this, "Old Straw Hat."

For buying useless goods at overinflated prices and using slipshod accounting methods he was eventually relieved of his job by a House of Representatives select committee on government contracts. The House implied that Cummings was a "well-meaning incompetent victimized by the circumstances of the emergency and duped by the contract profiteers who swarmed around War Department purchasers."

Cummings returned to Pennsylvania and recruited the 19th Pennsylvania Cavalry

and in October 1863, became its colonel.

Although the regiment saw action in the Trans-Mississippi in 1864, Cummings was not with them, having been detached to serve as Superintendent of Troops of African Descent for the State of Arkansas. He was able to organize one Black light artillery battery and five regiments of Black infantry. For his services during the war, Cummings was brevetted a brigadier general of Volunteers by President Andrew Johnson on April 19, 1865.

After the war the President appointed Cummings governor of the Territory of Colorado. Taking the oath on October 21, 1865, the next eighteen months were not very pleasant for Alexander Cummings. He was labeled as being "most unpopular" and "by nature and everything else as unfit for a governor as any man that ever lived." He was said to be, "stiff-necked, obstinate, willful and craftily able; an Aaron Burr in fertility of resource;..pig-headed and dictatorial to the last degree." His time in Colorado was said to be "of such a character as to cause the people of the Territory little desire to remember anything about him."

Twice during his administration Colorado statehood was passed by the Congress, only to be vetoed by President Johnson. Charges, among which was misdirecting monies, eventually compromised Cummings's ability to be a useful governor. Added to this was that even though evidence indicates Cummings "conscientiously tried to further the best interest of the territory," he ran up against a group of men who thought his interests were otherwise. Loosing any effectiveness that he might have had, he resigned the governorship in April 1867.

Cummings was appointed Collector of

Internal Revenue for the Fourth District of Pennsylvania and in July 1868, he was nominated for Commissioner of Internal Revenue. Rumors remaining from his days with the War Department dogged Cummings and despite the President's support, the Senate refused to confirm his appointment. Little information is available on Cummings's movement over the next few years. At some point he may have studied law as he later identifies himself as a "Councilor at Law." He was again given a government position during the Hayes administration when he was appointed as a Commercial Agent with the United States consular office in Ottawa, Canada. While performing his duties there, he died on July 16, 1879.

Cummings's obituary in the *Philadelphia Public Ledger* described him as "'energetic, ambitious, and restless,' and declared that he had merited better fortune than he had received." (BAM)

Cemetery Location: Section I, Lot 224

Inscription:
ALEXANDER CUMMINGS
BVT BRIG GEN
19 PENN CAV
NOV 17 1810
JUL 16 1879

Sources:
Hanchett, William. *"His Turbulent Excellency," Alexander Cummings, Governor of Colorado Territory, 1865-1867."* The *Colorado Magazine*, Volume 34 (April 1957).
Hunt, Roger D., and Jack R. Brown. *Brevet Brigadier Generals in Blue.* Gaithersburg. 1990.

John Adolph Bernard Dahlgren was born in Philadelphia on November 13, 1809. The son of the Swedish consul, Bernard Ulric Dahlgren, he was initially denied a midshipman's commission in the U.S. Navy. To gain experience he served for a time in the merchant service, finally being appointed as an acting midshipman aboard the frigate *Macedonian* in 1826. After serving in the Mediterranean and at the Philadelphia Naval Shipyard, Dahlgren was appointed to the Coast Survey in 1834. Promoted to lieutenant in March 1837, he returned to sea duty until eye trouble forced him to go on a leave of absence in 1843.

Transferred to the Washington Navy Yard in 1847, Dahlgren established and directed the Navy's ordnance department. During this time he was responsible for the invention of three types of ordnance; bronze boat howitzers and rifles, iron smoothbore shellguns, and iron rifles. "Dahlgren" guns, as they were to become known, were the most popular ordnance used by the federal and Confederate navies during the Civil War. Dahlgren was promoted to commander in October 1855.

On April 22, 1861, Dahlgren assumed command of the Washington Navy Yard when Francis Buchanan resigned to join the Confederacy. On July 16, 1862, he was promoted to captain and became chief of the Bureau of Ordnance two days later. Promoted to rear admiral in February 1863, Dahlgren applied for sea duty and in July received command of the South Atlantic Blockading Squadron. From August to October, the squadron bombarded Charleston, South Carolina's harbor defenses several times, but with little effect. In December 1864, the squadron supported General William T. Sherman in the capture of Savannah. Though Dahlgren showed himself to be a determined and effective commander, he was not especially gifted.

After the war, Dahlgren served as the commander of the South Pacific Squadron from 1866 to 1868. He was again the chief of the Bureau of Ordnance in 1868-1869, and the commandant of the Washington Navy Yard beginning in 1869. He died of heart disease, while on active duty, July 12, 1870. (BAM)

Cemetery Location: Section L, Lots 50-54.

Inscription: SACRED
TO THE MEMORY OF
MARY C. DAHLGREN
WIFE OF
J A DAHLGREN, U.S. NAVY
BORN IN PHILADELPHIA JULY 1817
AND DEPARTED THIS LIFE
WASHINGTON DC. JUNE 6, 1855
THE AFFECTIONATE WIFE, THE KIND
MOTHER
[?] DUTIFUL DAUGHTER, THE SINCERE
FRIEND
DIED AS SHE LIVED IN THE HOME OF
THE BLESSED
IMMORTALITY THROUGH THE MERCY
OF HER REDEEMER

JOHN ADOLPH DAHLGREN
REAR ADMIRAL U.S.N.
BORN NOV. 1809   DIED JULY 1870

Bronze Plaque:

REAR ADMIRAL JOHN ADOLPH
BERNARD DAHLGREN

UNITED STATES NAVY

SAILOR, SCIENTIST, SCHOLAR, TEACHER,
AUTHOR
"THE FATHER OF MODERN NAVAL
ORDNANCE"
HIS CONTRIBUTION TO THE DESIGN OF
NAVAL
ORDNANCE AND SHIP CONSTRUCTION
REVOLUTIONIZED THE NAVIES OF THE
WORLD
THIS MEMORIAL IS ERECTED ON
BEHALF OF A
GRATEFUL NAVY, BY THE OFFICERS
AND MEN OF
THE U.S.S. DAHLGREN, A GUIDED
MISSILE
FRIGATE, AND THE THIRD BRAVE SHIP
TO BEAR THIS
ILLUSTRIOUS NAME. DEDICATED
ON 15
APRIL 1961, IN THE CENTENNIAL YEAR
OF THE
WAR BETWEEN THE STATES, IN WHICH
REAR
ADMIRAL DAHLGREN SERVED THE
UNION FORCES
WITH DISTINCTION AS COMMANDER OF
THE
SOUTH ATLANTIC BLOCKADING
SQUADRON

Sources:
Appleton's Cyclopedia of American Biography (7 vols). New York. 1898.

Ulric Dahlgren was born in Neshaminy, Pennsylvania, on April 3, 1842. The son of Admiral John A. B. Dahlgren, Ulric moved to the Washington Naval Shipyard with his father in 1848. Attending local schools and receiving a practical education from the sailors at the shipyard, he became familiar with the construction and use of artillery. In 1858 he began the study of civil engineering and then, in 1860, he also began to study law.

At the beginning of the Civil War, Dahlgren returned to Washington, and after First Bull Run was detailed to take charge of a naval battery on Maryland Heights near Harpers Ferry, Virginia (now West Virginia). Dahlgren joined the staff of General Franz Sigel and served during General John C. Frémont's mountain campaign and General John Pope's 1862 campaign.

At the battle of Second Bull Run, Ulric was the chief of artillery for Sigel. After leading a raid on Fredericksburg, he was rewarded for his gallantry by being detailed as a special aide on the staff of General Ambrose Burnside. Later detailed to General Joseph Hooker's staff, Dahlgren performed well during the Chancellorsville Campaign.

As part of General George Meade's staff, Dahlgren again distinguished himself in the Gettysburg Campaign. During General Robert E. Lee's retreat to Virginia, Dahlgren led a detail of men in an attempt to harass the Confederate column. Participating in a cavalry charge in Hagerstown, Maryland, on July 6, he was severely wounded in the foot, necessitating amputation of his leg. (Dahlgren's leg is buried in the wall of Building No. 28 on the grounds of the Washington Navy Yard, in Washington, D.C. A plaque on the building states: "Within this wall is deposited the leg of Col. Ulric Dahlgren, USV, wounded July 6, 1863, while skirmishing in the streets of Hagerstown with the rebels after the Battle of Gettysburg.") After his recovery he was promoted to colonel and returned to duty in February 1864.

Shortly after returning to duty, Dahlgren participated in a raid on Richmond, as part of a force led by General H. Judson Kilpatrick. The purpose of the raid was to capture Richmond and free prisoners at Libby Prison and Belle Island. Kilpatrick, with the main force, was to attack the city from the north, while Dahlgren, with a satellite force, would enter the city from the west.

The raid was a disaster. Swollen streams, snow, sleet, and unexpected Confederate troops, caused the federal forces to withdraw. On March 2, Dahlgren and 100 of his men became surrounded near King and Queen's Court House. During the fighting, Dahlgren was killed and the rest of his command was captured. Papers reputedly found on Dahlgren's body indicated the purpose of the raid was to kill Jefferson Davis and the Confederate cabinet. Denial of these papers set off a debate which is yet to be resolved.

Dahlgren's little finger was cut off to steal a ring while his artificial leg was taken and given to a maimed Confederate soldier. (Both these items were recovered in late 1865.) Buried where he fell, (now called Dahlgren's Corner) his body was later moved to an unmarked grave in Richmond. The body was dug up and buried two more times before local Unionists retrieved it and transported it into federal lines near Frederick's Hall where, once again, it was buried. After the war, Admiral Dahlgren finally retrieved the body of his son and moved it to Philadelphia. Today, Ulric Dahlgren lies next to his parents in Laurel Hill. (BAM)

Cemetery Location: Section L, Lots 50-54.

Inscription:

COL. ULRIC DAHLGREN
U.S. ARMY
KILLED MARCH 2, 1864
21 YEARS 11 MO.

Sources:
Appleton's Cyclopedia of American Biography (7 vols). New York. 1898.
Boatner, Mark Mayo, III. *The Civil War Dictionary*. New York. 1958.

Faust, Patricia L. *Historical Times Illustrated Encyclopedia of the Civil War.* New York. 1986.

Forman, Stephen M. *A Guide to Civil War Washington.* Washington. 1995.

Furgurson, Ernest B. *Ashes of Glory: Richmond at War.* New York. 1996.

Percival Drayton was born in South Carolina on August 25, 1812. He entered the navy as a midshipman on December 1, 1827, and was promoted to lieutenant on February 28, 1838, serving in the Brazilian, Mediterranean, and Pacific squadrons. He served at the Naval Observatory in Washington, on the Paraguay expedition of 1858, and at the beginning of the Civil War was on duty at the Philadelphia Navy Yard.

Drayton remained loyal to the Union, although his brother became a Confederate brigadier general. Percival became the commander of the *Pocahontas* which successfully attacked the Confederate forts at Port Royal, commanded by his brother. He was promoted to captain on July 16, 1862, and placed in command of the *Passaic*.

Promoted to command of the West Gulf Squadron, Drayton commanded Admiral David Farragut's flag-ship, the USS *Hartford*, in the battle of Mobile Bay on August 5, 1864. Farragut spoke highly of Drayton indicating that he was "a man of determined energy, untiring devotion to duty, and zeal..."

After the war Captain Drayton became Chief of the Bureau of Navigation. He died while on duty on August 4, 1865. (BAM)

Cemetery Location: Section G, Lot 249.

Inscription:
PERCIVAL DRAYTON
CAPTAIN U.S. NAVY
BORN AUGUST 25, 1812
DIED AUGUST 4, 1865

Sources: Cemetery Records, Laurel Hill Cemetery, Philadelphia, PA.

Charles Ellet, Jr., was born on January 1, 1810, at Penn's Manor, Bucks County,

Pennsylvania, the sixth child of Charles and Mary Ellet. Known throughout his life as Charles, Jr., he would become an ambitious civil engineer, accomplishing many engineering feats. However, it would be his invention of the "Steam Rams," an idea he had in the 1850s, which would be his greatest accomplishment. After the destruction caused by the CSS *Virginia* in early March 1862, Secretary of War Edwin Stanton sent a dispatch to Ellet, instructing him to proceed to Pittsburgh, Cincinnati, and New Albany, "to provide Steam rams for the defense against iron clad vessels on the Western waters."

Ellet was commissioned colonel and would complete the task of building his "Ram Fleet" out of nine old steam boats, in just under fifty days. Assigned as an aide-de-camp to General John C. Frémont on April 28, 1862, he would set out to prove that his idea would work. The Mississippi River was the key to the Confederacy, and if it could be controlled, the South would be split in two.

The Mississippi Ram Fleet (as the Steam Rams were to become known), consisted of nine rams, including *The Queen of the West*, under the command of Charles Ellet and the *Monarch*, under Alfred Ellet, with three other members of the Ellet family, including Charles's son Charles Rivers Ellet, as a medical cadet, attached. The Ram Fleet was an all volunteer organization and had the advantage of speed and toughness, but lacked armor and were not heavily gunned.

On June 6, 1862, the fleet engaged the Confederate Defense Fleet just above Memphis, Tennessee. When most of the Defense Fleet had been sunk or forced to retreat, the city of Memphis surrendered to the Ram fleet. During the action, Colonel Ellet was shot in the knee with a pistol bullet. While he laid on the deck he continued to give orders to the Rams and at one point told Alfred to "stand by his post."

The Colonel had never enjoyed a robust health and a recent bout with the measles had sapped his strength. Although it was thought he would recover from his wound, he died on June 21. His body was transported back to Philadelphia and taken to Independence Hall, where it would lie in state. On June 27, the funeral for Ellet was held with the Keystone Artillerists acting as honor guard. Ellet's wife was so stricken with grief that she died eight days later.

On June 11, 1938, a new ship was launched from Kearny, New Jersey. The ship was commissioned the USS *Ellet*, DD 398, named for the five Ellets who served with the Mississippi Ram Fleet. The ship would have its own share of glory, earning ten battle stars, a credit to the Ellet name. (DH)

Cemetery Location: Section C, Lot 12.

Inscription:
SACRED
TO THE MEMORY OF
CHARLES ELLET JR
COMMANDING MISSISSIPPI RAM FLEET
AND OF ELVIRA HIS WIFE
[unreadable]
[unreadable]

Sources:
Service Record, National Archives.

Faust, Patricia L. *Historical Times Illustrated Encyclopedia of the Civil War.* New York. 1986.

Johnson, Allen, and Dumas Malone (eds). *Dictionary of American Biography.* (11 vols.). New York. 1946.

Johnson, Robert U., and Clarence C. Buel. *Battles and Leaders of the Civil War.* (4 vols.). New York. 1887.

Charles Rivers Ellet was born in Georgetown, D.C., on July 1, 1843. He was the son of Colonel Charles Ellet and his wife Elvira. At the age of nineteen, Charles joined his father as a medical cadet with the Mississippi Ram Fleet. After the surrender of Memphis, Tennessee, on June 6, 1862, it was young Charles who would raise "Old Glory" over the city. In doing so, he risked personal injury from a hostile crowd. On November 5, 1862, he was promoted to colonel, the youngest person to ever hold that rank in the Union army.

As the campaign along the Mississippi

River and Vicksburg, Mississippi, progressed, the Ram Fleet became a valuable tool to both General U.S. Grant, and acting Rear Admiral David Porter. The Rams were in a unique situation, being "in" the army, but subject to the orders of the navy. In February 1863, Ellet, in command of *The Queen of the West*, started up river past Vicksburg

toward Port Hudson, Mississippi, in order to create trouble with Confederate shipping. While steaming up the Red River, the *Queen* was run aground by a river pilot of questionable loyalty. Ellet and the crew were forced to abandon the boat and head back down the river on a captured steamer.

Colonel Ellet became the second in command of the Mississippi Marine Brigade and on March 22, 1863, was involved in actions at Milliken's Bend, Louisiana, and the burning of Austin, Mississippi. However, brigade problems and failing health forced him to resign his commission on September 8, 1863. Ellet contracted typhoid fever and went to Bunker Hill, Illinois, where he died on October 29, 1863. His body was transported back to Philadelphia, to lie with his mother and father at Laurel Hill. (DH)

Cemetery Location: Section C, Lot 12.

Inscription:
COLONEL
CHARLES RIVERS ELLET
[unreadable]
[unreadable]
[unreadable]
BORN JULY 1 1843
DIED OCTOBER 29 1863

Sources:
Service Record, National Archives.
Westwood, Howard C. "The Ellet Family Fleet." *Civil War Times Illustrated.* (October 1982).

Benezet Forst Foust was born in Philadelphia, Pennsylvania, on April 5, 1840. Raised in a wealthy family, he studied law, and by the outbreak of the Civil War was described as a "promising young lawyer." In August 1861, he enlisted in the newly formed Cameron Light Guards and on October 3, he was mustered into service as adjutant of the 88th Pennsylvania Volunteers. At the time of his enlistment, twenty-one-year-old

Benezet was six feet tall, with blue eyes and light brown hair.

During the first six months of its service, the 88th saw little action, serving mostly as provost guards in and around Alexandria, Virginia. However, during the spring and summer of 1862, the 88th fought in the Shenandoah Valley at Cedar Mountain and lost almost half their men at the disastrous battle of Second Bull Run. On September 17, at the battle of Antietam, the regiment again suffered severe casualties in the savage struggle for Miller's cornfield.

The losses in officers during these battles had been especially high. As a result, on November 28, 1862, Foust was promoted to captain of Company A. On December 13, at the battle of Fredericksburg he received "particular" mention in the official report of his regimental commander for his "noble conduct" in helping to rally his men. On New Year's Eve 1862, Captain Foust was promoted to major. Because the regimental commander was still suffering from his wounds received at Second Bull Run, Major Foust would command the regiment through most of the winter and spring of 1863. On July 1, 1863, Major Foust led the 88th onto the battlefield of Gettysburg where "soon after the beginning of the fight" he "received a shell wound in the right breast." He was ordered to his home in Philadelphia, where suffering from a chest contusion, internal bleeding, and partial paralysis of the right arm, he was unable to fully recover from his wound.

On November 7, 1863, he resigned his commission and was transferred to the Veteran Reserve Corps where he would eventually obtain the rank of lieutenant colonel in the 10th Regiment. During 1864 and 1865 his duties involved garrisoning the forts around Washington and office work at the War Department.

On March 13, 1865, Foust was breveted brigadier general for his "gallant and meritorious service at the battles of Fredericksburg, Chancellorsville, Gettysburg, Cedar Mountain, Mitchell's Station, Rappahannock Station, White Sulphur Springs, and Thoroughfare Gap." He was honorably discharged on January 1, 1868, at Baltimore, Maryland.

He returned to his home in Philadelphia and in August 1869, filed for an invalid pension, complaining that he was unable to work because he had contracted bronchitis and was suffering from an infection of the lungs as a result of his Gettysburg wound. He would not live to receive a pension however, as on January 8, 1870, "after a lingering disease" Benezet Foust died at the age of thirty, a forgotten casualty of the battle of Gettysburg. (THS)

Cemetery Location: Section Y, Lot 84.

Inscription:
> In Memoriam
> Brig. Gen.
> Benezet F. Foust
> son of
> R.M. & H.N. Foust
> Born April 5, 1840
> Died Jan. 8, 1870
> [unreadable]
>
> FOUST

Sources:
Bates, Samuel P. *History of Pennsylvania Volunteers*. (5 vols). Harrisburg. 1869.
Census Record of the United States, 1860, Philadelphia.
Hunt, Roger D., and Jack R. Brown. *Brevet Brigadier Generals in Blue*. Gaithersburg. 1990.
Obituary of Benezet F. Foust, Philadelphia *Inquirer*, January 10, 1870.
Pennsylvania. Gettysburg Battlefield Commission, *Pennsylvania at Gettysburg. Ceremonies at the Dedication of the Monuments Erected by the Commonwealth of Pennsylvania to Mark the Positions of the Pennsylvania Commands Engaged in the Battle*. Harrisburg. 1904.
Pension and Service Record of Benezet F. Foust. National Archives. Washington.
U.S. Department of War. *The War of the Rebellion: A Compilation of the Official Records of the Union and Confederate Armies*. (128 vols). Washington. 1880-1901.
Vautier, John D. *History of the 88th Pennsylvania Volunteers in the War for the Union*. Philadelphia. 1894.

Louis Raymond Francine was born on March 26, 1837, in Philadelphia. He was the oldest son of Jacques Louis de

Francine, a French emigre who's family members served posts of honor and trust in France. Young Louis lived the early part of his years in Camden, New Jersey, attending private schools and later a military school in Flushing, Long Island. In 1851, Francine went to France to finish his education. Attending the famous Ecole Polytechnique in Paris and the French Army training school for officers and engineers, Louis did well in his studies. Meanwhile, back in America where dark clouds of war began to bloom, Louis saw an opportunity for military service.

Returning to New Jersey, Francine took up the task, along with George W. Smith, a Cape May resident, of raising a company which became Company "A" 7th New Jersey Volunteer Infantry. Francine was made a captain and went about the duty of drilling the company to get them ready for the war. The 7th left Camp Olden in Trenton, for Washington, D.C., on September 19, 1861, and later became part of the "Second New Jersey Brigade." The 7th and Captain Francine saw action at Yorktown, Williamsburg, White Oak Swamp, Seven Pines, the Seven Days, Second Bull Run, Chantilly, and Centreville. On December 8, 1862, Francine became regimental lieutenant colonel and then the next day, colonel. The regiment took part in Fredericksburg and Chancellorsville, where it captured five Confederate flags and almost 500 prisoners.

At Gettysburg the 7th was part of the Third Corps where, on July 2, it was positioned in support of Clark's Battery (Battery "B" 1st N.J. Artillery) in the Peach Orchard. The gallant 7th and their Colonel were under fire by both musketry and shell until forced to retire with the rest of the Corps. Not wanting to leave the field, the 7th waited until they could fire at the advancing Confederates, a point of honor. It was here that Colonel Francine received his mortal wound. Shot in the hip, he laid on the field and was later removed to Philadelphia where he died on July 16.

On April 29, 1867, the Francine family received the news that Louis would be breveted brigadier general of U.S. Volunteers for "gallant and meritorious service at the battle of Gettysburg, PA where he was mortally wounded." On June 30, 1888, the 7th New Jersey Monument was dedicated at Gettysburg. The monument, a large "Minie Ball," has

a granite base with inscriptions around it. One of these states, "Here Col. Francine Fell." (DH)

Cemetery Location: Section Y, Lot 44.

Inscription:
> Louis R. Francine
> Colonel of the
> 7th Regt. New Jersey Vols.
> Who after serving with honor
> in the Battles of Yorktown
> Williamsburg Malvern Hill
> Briston Manassas [unreadable]
> Chantilly Fredericksburg
> and Chancellorsville
> was mortally wounded at the
> Battle of Gettysburg
> July 2nd 1863
> in the 26th year of his age
> Jesu Hominum Salvator

Sources:
Service Record, National Archives.
Francine, Albert P. "Louis Raymond Francine Brevet Brigadier General U. S. Volunteers," Philadelphia. 1910.

Sylvanus William Godon was born in Philadelphia on June 18, 1809. He was appointed a midshipman at the age of ten and was eventually promoted to lieutenant in 1836. Godon served on the *Ohio* under Commodore Isaac Hull in the Mediterranean during the years 1839, 1840, and 1841. During the Mexican War he was present at Vera Cruz. He was promoted to commander in 1835 and then captain in 1861.

During the Civil War Godon commanded the *Mohican* which took part in the attack on Port Royal as part of Admiral Samuel DuPont's fleet. He was also part of the fleet which bombarded

Hilton Head, SC. In 1863, Godon was promoted to commodore and commanded the fourth division of Admiral David D. Porter's fleet at Fort Fisher, NC, in December 1864 and January 1865. At the close of the war he was promoted to rear-admiral.

Following the Civil War, Godon was commandant of the Brooklyn Navy Yard from 1868 to 1870. He was promoted to the rank of rear-admiral on July 25, 1866. He retired due to old age on June 18, 1871. Godon was a widower who had no children. He died in Blois, France, on May 17, 1879. (BAM)

Cemetery Location: Section F, Lot 14.

Inscription:
> SYLVANUS WILLIAM GODON
> REAR ADMIRAL US NAVY
> DIED AT BLOIS FRANCE
> MAY 17 1879

Source:
Cogar, William B. *Dictionary of Admirals of the U.S. Navy, Volume 1, 1862-1900.* Annapolis. 1989.
Cemetery Records. Laurel Hill Cemetery, Philadelphia, PA.

Edgar Mantlebert Gregory was born in Sand Lake, New York, on January 1, 1804. He married Ellen Young of Deposit, New York, and they had three children. The couple moved to Cincinnati, Ohio, where Gregory participated in the lumber, banking, and railroad business. During this time he assisted runaway slaves in escaping to Canada. At some point before the Civil War he transferred his business to Philadelphia.

At the outbreak of the war Gregory recruited the 91st Pennsylvania Infantry of which he became colonel. Gregory, his two sons, and the 91st served continuously from December 1861 to the end of the war. The regiment participated in twenty-one engagements and was present during the surrender at Appomattox. Gregory had five horses killed under him and received a leg wound at Chancellorsville that would ultimately cause his death. He was brevetted brigadier general on September 30, 1864, for "gallant and distinguished services" at Poplar Spring Church, Virginia. During the Appomattox Campaign he commanded the Second Brigade, First Division, Fifth Corps. He was brevetted again to major general on August 9, 1866, for "gallant conduct" at the battle of Five Forks, Virginia.

After the war Gregory served as the first Assistant Commissioner of the Freedmen's Bureau in Texas. He felt that the former slaves should be assimilated into postbellum society, but he faced strong opposition from the planter class and eventually succumbed to a smear campaign by antebellum state politicians and former slaver holders. He was relieved of his position, returned to Philadelphia, and later became a United States Marshal. Gregory was a Republican, Presbyterian, and a Mason. He died in Philadelphia on November 7, 1871. (BAM)

Cemetery Location: Section 16, Lot 313

Inscription:
> EDGAR M GREGORY
> BVT BRIG GEN
> 91 PA INF
> JAN 1 1804
> NOV 7 1871

Sources:
Hunt, Roger D., and Jack R. Brown. *Brevet Brigadier Generals in Blue.* Gaithersburg. 1990.
Gregory, Grant. *Ancestors and Descendants of Henry Gregory.* Provincetown. 1938.
Richter, William L. *Overreached On All Sides: The Freedmen's Bureau Administration in Texas, 1865-1868.* College Station. 1991.

Caldwell Keppele Hall was born in Philadelphia, on March 10, 1839, the son of Rev. John Hall, D. D. The family moved to Trenton, New Jersey, in 1841 where Hall was educated at nearby Princeton University, graduating in 1857. At the outbreak of the Civil War he was a practicing attorney in Trenton.

Hall joined the 5th New Jersey on August 28, 1861, as regimental adjutant. He later became the Assistant Adjutant General on the staff of General Joseph B. Carr. When General Francis Patterson succeeded to command of the brigade, Hall became an aide-de-camp. After serving at Williamsburg and during the Peninsula Campaign, Hall was relieved from duty. On August 25, 1862, he accepted the position of lieutenant colonel in the 14th New Jersey. The regiment served on picket duty until joining the Army of the Potomac just before the battle of Gettysburg.

The 14th participated in all of the battles of the Army of the Potomac until its term of service ended. Hall received a wound during the battle of Monocacy in July 1864, and was hospitalized in Baltimore. Due to the disability caused by his wounds he was honorably discharged on September 10, 1864. On March 13, 1865, he was breveted brigadier general for "gallant service at the battle of the Monocacy, Md."

Hall resumed the practice of law in Trenton and in February 1867, was appointed the Prosecutor of the Pleas for Mercer County. He held this post until his death from consumption on May 30, 1870. (BAM)

Inscription:
CALDWELL K HALL
BVT BRIG GEN
14 NJ INF
MAR 10 1839
MAY 30 1870

Sources:
Hunt, Roger D., and Jack R. Brown. *Brevet Brigadier Generals in Blue*. Gaithersburg. 1990.
Obituary, *Trenton Daily State Gazette*, May 31, 1870.

Cemetery Location: Section G, Lot 245.

John William Hofmann was born in Philadelphia, on February 18, 1824. Before the Civil War he was engaged in the mercantile business and was one of, if not the, leading hosiery merchants in Philadelphia. He was active in the local militia as a member of the "Junior Artillerists" and the Washington Grays, taking part in the riots of 1842-44.

At the outbreak of the Civil War, Hofmann became the captain of Company E, 23rd Pennsylvania Volunteers. When the regiment was mustered out after its three months service, he became lieutenant colonel of the 56th Pennsylvania Volunteers and for a time was in command of Camp Curtain near Harrisburg. In early 1862, the regiment was attached to the Army of Virginia and then the Army of the Potomac. During this time Hofmann served with distinction spending most of his time in command of a brigade. On August 1, 1864, he was breveted brigadier general, USV, for "brave, consistent and efficient services in the battles and marches of the campaign."

After the war, Hofmann was twice commissioned brigadier general and commanded the Second Brigade, First Division, Pennsylvania National Guard, located in Philadelphia. At the time of his death on March 5, 1902, he was a member of a number of military organizations including the "Old Guard" Artillery Corps and Washington Grays. (BAM)

Cemetery Location: Section G, Lot 63.

Inscription: [unreadable]

Sources:
Hofmann File. Cemetery Records. Laurel Hill Cemetery. Philadelphia, PA. Hunt, Roger D., and Jack R. Brown. *Brevet Brigadier Generals in Blue.* Gaithersburg. 1990.

Oliver Blachly Knowles was born in Philadelphia, on January 3, 1842. He was son of Levi Knowles, a Philadelphia merchant, and Elizabeth Adeline Croskey. Knowles attended local public schools and spent two years in high school before entering his father's business. At an early age he showed a strong predilection for horses and became a good rider.

At the outbreak of the war, Knowles enlisted as a private in the First New York (Lincoln) Cavalry. The regiment's first action was near Pohick Church, Virginia, where during a sharp skirmish, Knowles showed his coolness, intelligence, and courage. For his gallantry he was promoted to corporal in September 1861, but only after being forced to do so by his captain. The following January he was again promoted, this time to orderly sergeant and then to second lieutenant for distinguished gallantry at the close of the Peninsula Campaign. A fellow officer commented of Knowles: "He was never sick, always ready for duty, and seemed to regard the most fatiguing service or hazardous undertaking as pastime."

The regiment participated in the Antietam Campaign and was then assigned to the command of General Robert Milroy stationed in the Shenandoah Valley and along the Potomac River. He was commissioned first lieutenant in April 1863, and after returning early from a well deserved furlough, Knowles joined his regiment in Harrisburg and participated in the Gettysburg Campaign.

Knowles went on to become major of the 21st Pennsylvania Cavalry, which served as infantry during part of the 1864 Overland Campaign and the siege of Petersburg. In October 1864, Knowles was promoted to colonel and the regiment was remounted and attached to the cavalry corps of General David McM. Gregg.

The regiment participated in the actions south of Petersburg and the final campaign to Appomattox Court House. Shortly after the end of the war, Knowles was promoted to brevet brigadier general to date from March 13, 1865, for meritorious services during the war.

On the 4th of July Knowles was mustered out of service. Returning to Philadelphia he eventually settled in Milwaukee, Wisconsin, and participated in the grain trade. On December 5, 1866, Knowles was stricken with cholera and died within five hours. The six foot two inch, well proportioned, and fair complected Knowles was only twenty-five-years-old. (BAM)

Cemetery Location: Section K, Lot 106.

Inscription: Oliver B. Knowles
[?] 21st Penna Cav [?]
[?] Gen. [?]
Died Dec. 5, 1866
Age 25 years
[unreadable*]

* The unreadable inscription once read:

He Was:
Gentle, yet Courageous,
Firm, but Magnanimous,
Beloved by all

Sources:
Bates, Samuel P. *Martial Deeds of Pennsylvania*. Philadelphia. 1875.
Hunt, Roger D., and Jack R. Brown. *Brevet Brigadier Generals in Blue*. Gaithersburg. 1990.

William David Lewis, Jr. was born in Philadelphia on May 19, 1827, the only son of William David and Sarah Claypoole Lewis. He married Clara Fasset in 1852 and they had one child, William David, III, who died in less than a year. Before the war Lewis made his living in the coal business and was active in the local militia.

In 1861, at the initial call for volunteers, Lewis served as the colonel of the 18th Pennsylvania, a three-month unit which was mustered out in August. In October he became the colonel of the 110th Pennsylvania Infantry, distinguishing himself at the battle of Winchester (March 23, 1862) and Port Republic (June 8, 1862). He resigned due to disabilities on December 23, 1862, and on March 13, 1865, he was brevetted brigadier general for "gallant and meritorious services in the field during the war."

After the war, Lewis became a man of leisure. Never fully recovering his health after his military service, Lewis died in Philadelphia on January 19, 1872. (BAM)

Cemetery Location: Section A, Lots 91-102.

27

Inscription:
> In Memory of
> William D. Lewis, Jr.
> Brev. Brig. Gen. Vol.
> Born May 19, 1827
> Died Jan. 19, 1872

Sources:
Appleton's Cyclopedia of American Biography (7 vols.). New York. 1891.
Hunt, Roger D., and Jack R. Brown. *Brevet Brigadier Generals in Blue.* Gaithersburg. 1990.

George Gordon Meade was born in Cadiz, Spain, on December 31, 1815. His father, Richard Worsham Meade, was a wealthy merchant and U.S. Navy agent who had lent substantial sums of money to the Spanish government. At the end of the Napoleonic Wars, the elder Meade found himself in prison for pressing to strenuously for repayment. Only action by the administration in Washington, D.C., freed him.

In June 1816, at the age of one and a half, George and his mother returned to the United States and Philadelphia where the family had roots. He attended a Philadelphia elementary school then a military academy in near-by Germantown. The rest of the family had moved to Washington, D.C. with his father, who was still attempting to recover the money that he had lost in Spain. Upon his father's death in 1828, George was forced to withdraw from the academy, move to Washington, and attend a small school conducted by Salmon P. Chase. Later, after attending the Mount Hope Institution in Baltimore, George received an appointment to the Military Academy at West Point.

Graduating in 1835, nineteenth in a class of fifty-three, Meade became a second lieutenant in the 3rd Artillery. After seeing service in the Seminole War in Florida and then at the Watertown (Massachusetts) Arsenal, he resigned his commission on October 26, 1836, to pursue a career in civil engineering. He worked for a time in Florida, and then on a survey of the Mississippi and Texas borders. On December 31, 1840, Meade married Margaretta Seargent, the daughter of Congressman John Sergeant, who had been helpful in getting his father freed from a Spanish jail.

On May 19, 1842, Meade rejoined the army as a second lieutenant in the Corps of Topographical Engineers. After completing a survey of the northeastern border in Maine, he was transferred to Philadelphia to work on lighthouse construction in the Delaware Bay. In August 1845, Meade was transferred to the command of Zachary Taylor in Corpus Christi, Texas. During the Mexican War, Meade served at Palo Alto and Resaca de la Palma. After the battle of Monterey he was brevetted a first lieutenant for bravery. Following the war Meade returned to his duties as an engineer in the construction of lighthouses and breakwaters, and the surveys of coastal and inland waters.

The outbreak of the Civil War found Meade a captain working on harbors along the Great Lakes. At the urging of Pennsylvania Governor Andrew Curtain, Meade was made a brigadier general and placed in command of a brigade of Pennsylvania Reserves. Meade and his brigade spent the winter in the defenses of Washington where they participated in the construction of Fort Pennsylvania. During this time, Meade paid $150 for a horse named "Old Baldy," whose gait was so fast that aides had a difficult time keeping up with him.

In March 1862, Meade's command was transferred to Major General Irvin McDowell's army. The Reserves eventually moved to Falmouth, Virginia, where Meade could do little but drill the men and participate in dress parades. Finally in June, Meade and his regiments were transferred to the Virginia peninsula. Here, under the command of Major General George B. McClellan, the brigade took part in the battles of Mechanicsville, Gaines's Mill, and Glendale. At Glendale, while urging his men forward, Meade was seriously wounded when he was hit in the arm and the hip. Forced to leave the field, he eventually returned to his family in Philadelphia to recuperate.

Failing to take time for a full recovery, Meade was back in command of his troops at Second Bull Run. Placed in temporary command of Reynolds's Division of Hooker's First Corps, he participated in the fighting at South Mountain. At Antietam he courageously led his men, assuming command of the First Corps

upon the wounding of Hooker. Meade returned to division command and along with the rest of the Army of the Potomac moved back into camp in Falmouth, just across the Rappahannock River from Fredericksburg.

On November 29, 1862, Meade was promoted to major general of volunteers. As part of Franklin's "Left Grand Division" at Fredericksburg, his men were able to temporarily pierce Jackson's Confederate line before being thrown back with considerable losses. On December 25, Meade took over command of the Fifth Corps. Participating in the fighting at Chancellorsville in May 1863, Meade's Corps performed well, being the first on the field and the last to leave, covering the federal rear.

Lee's success against the federal army prompted the Confederate government to opt for an invasion of Northern territory. Lincoln, on the other hand, was trying to find a general who could lead the Army of the Potomac and win. The month of June saw the two great armies inching their way northward. On June 28, Meade and his Fifth Corps were encamped just outside of Frederick, Maryland. In the predawn hours Meade received a visit from Major James Hardie with General Order 191, placing the General in command of the Army of the Potomac. Having no choice but to accept, Meade commented, "Well, I've been tried and condemned without a hearing, and I suppose I shall have to go to the execution."

Within three days Meade and his army were engaged in the greatest battle ever fought on American soil, the battle of Gettysburg. For three days the Army of Northern Virginia threw its regiments against Meade's right, left, and then center. Meade handled his army well, eventually forcing Lee to retreat. Slow to follow, due to exhaustion and casualties, he was criticized for allowing Lee's army to escape back into Virginia. When told of Lincoln's "dissatisfaction," Meade offered his resignation, which was not accepted. Rather, he was promoted to brigadier general in the Regular Army to date from July 3, 1863. The next few months were taken up by the indecisive Bristoe Station and Mine Run campaigns. On January 28, 1864, Meade received the thanks of Congress for his actions at Gettysburg.

In the spring of 1864, Ulysses S. Grant was promoted to lieutenant general and placed in command of all Union forces. Grant opted to place his headquarters with the Army of the Potomac, thus causing an awkward command arrangement. Though Meade remained in command of the army, his leadership was somewhat preempted by Grant's presence. He was with the army though the 1864 Overland Campaign, the siege of Petersburg, and until the surrender of the Army of Northern Virginia at Appomattox Court House in April 1865. On August 18, 1864, Meade was promoted to major general in the Regular Army.

After the war Meade was placed in command of the Military Division of the Atlantic and the Department of the East in Philadelphia. In 1868, he was sent by President Johnson to administer Reconstruction Policy in Georgia. He later returned to Philadelphia where he resumed his duties in the Department of the East and enjoyed a tranquil existence in his domestic life and as part of Philadelphia society. The proud citizens of the city presented him with a house which today sits at 1836 Delancy Place.

On November 2, 1872, Meade complained of being ill and was forced to bed. Suffering from pneumonia, the General's condition worsened. At 6:00 p.m. on November 7, Meade died, just two months short of his fifty-seventh birthday. After an impressive funeral service at St. Mark's Episcopal Church on Locust Street, the cortege wound its way though the hushed streets to the Schuylkill River. Meade's faithful horse "Old Baldy" was brought out of retirement and followed the General's casket. In attendance were President Grant, General Sherman, the Governor of Pennsylvania, members of the Cabinet as well as other dignitaries and thousands of Meade's former soldiers. George Gordon Meade was taken to Laurel Hill Cemetery and laid to rest. (BAM)

Cemetery Location: Section L, Lots 1-7.

Inscription:
George Gordon Meade
Major General U. S. Army
Born at Cadiz, Spain
Dec. 31, 1815

Died at Philadelphia
Nov. 6, 1872
He did his work bravely
and is at rest

Sources:
Appleton's Cyclopedia of American Biography (7 vols.). New York. 1898.
Meade File. Cemetery Records. Laurel Hill Cemetery. Philadelphia, PA.
Warner, Ezra. *Generals in Blue: Lives of the Union Commanders.* Baton Rouge. 1964.

George Gordon Meade, Jr. was born in Philadelphia on November 2, 1843. He entered the United States Military Academy at West Point on July 1, 1860. Having enlisted as a private in the 8th Pennsylvania Infantry in 1861, Meade joined the unit after resigning as a cadet on June 21, 1862, and served with it throughout the Antietam Campaign. He was honorably discharged from the unit in September 1862.

A month later, Meade was appointed second lieutenant in the 6th Pennsylvania Cavalry (Rush's Lancers). After serving with the regiment through the Fredericksburg Campaign and General George Stoneman's raids of April and May 1863, Meade was appointed captain and aide-de-camp to serve on his father's staff. General Meade was destined to be appointed commander of the Army of the Potomac just days later. Meade remained a member of his father's staff throughout the rest of the war and received two brevet promotions as a volunteer; to major, on August 1, 1864, "for faithful and meritorious service in the field," and to lieutenant colonel, "for gallant and meritorious services during the recent operations resulting in the fall of Richmond, Virginia, and the surrender of the insurgent army under General R. E. Lee." In 1867, Meade also received similar brevet promotions in the Regular Army. Following the war Meade remained in the army and rose to the rank of captain. Although he was at various times assigned to the First Artillery, and the 22nd and 31st Infantry regiments, he once again spent most of the time on his father's staff.

In 1874, Meade resigned his commission and became a stock broker in Philadelphia. He became active in a number of patriotic organizations and spent much time and energy defending his father's actions following the battle of Gettysburg.

After suffering from kidney problems for more than two months, Meade died at his home at 1216 Walnut Street, Philadelphia at 4 p.m. on February 2, 1897, at the age of fifty-three. Funeral services for Colonel Meade took place at St. Luke's Church, 13th and Spruce Streets, and he was buried at Laurel Hill in a private ceremony. (SJW)

Cemetery Location: Section 10, Lots 21 & 50.

Inscription:
GEORGE MEADE
BORN NOVEMBER 2, 1843
DIED FEBRUARY 2, 1897
AND
BESSIE LEWIS MEADE
HIS WIFE
BORN APRIL 10, 1849
DIED JULY 5, 1931

Sources:
George Gordon Meade, Jr., entry, Pennsylvania Commandery Scrapbooks (Scrapbook 20, # 915). The Civil War Library and Museum, Philadelphia, PA.

Samuel Mercer was born in Maryland (circa. 1799) and was commissioned a midshipman in the U.S. Navy on March 4, 1815. He served in various shore positions and had a total of over nineteen years of service at sea when the Civil War opened in 1861.

During the Mexican War he had commanded the *Lawrence*, a 10-gun brig, as part of the Home Squadron. Promoted to commander on September 14, 1855, Mercer was the commanding officer of the *Powhatan*, an 11-gun sidewheel sloop, when Confederate forces began threatening Union forces at Fort Sumter, located in Charleston, South Carolina, harbor.

In early April 1861, he was sent to command a naval force (*Powhatan*, *Pawnee*, *Pocahontas*, and the revenue cutter *Harriet Lane*), to relieve the garrison at Fort Sumter. The squadron arrived a day too late, as the Confederate bombardment had begun forcing the surrender of the fort and precipitating the Civil War.

Mercer returned to Charleston harbor in May, commanding the 40-gun steam frigate *Wabash*, as part of the Northern Atlantic Blockading Squadron. He participated in the successful joint army-navy expedition against the forts at Cape Hatteras, North Carolina, in August 1861. The *Wabash* was later damaged by Confederate cannon fire and was sent to New York for repairs.

Upon arrival, Captain Mercer was relieved of active command and appointed to the Navy Retiring Board. He died in Brooklyn, New York, on March 6, 1862, at age sixty-three.

His funeral was held from the home of his brother-in-law (with "male friends invited to attend") at 248 West Logan

Square in Philadelphia on Saturday, March 8, 1862, with burial following at Laurel Hill. (PEP)

[Editor's note: No photograph of Samuel Mercer was found.]

Cemetery Location: Section L, Lot 185.

Inscription:

COMMODORE SAMUEL MERCER
USN 1799---
[Remainder of marker buried]

Sources:
Philadelphia *Inquirer*, March 17, 1862.
Register of the Commissioned, Warrant, and Volunteer Officers of the Navy of the United States. Washington, D.C. Various years.
Spears, John R. *The History of Our Navy From Its Origin to the Present Day, 1775-1897*. New York. 1897.

James St. Clair Morton was born in Philadelphia on September 24, 1829. After attending the University of Pennsylvania, he entered West Point where he graduated in 1851, second in a class of forty-two. Entering the Engineering Corps, he participated in a number of projects, including assignments at Charleston Harbor, Fort Delaware, and Fort Hancock. From 1855 to 1857, he served as an assistant professor of engineering at the Military Academy. In 1860 Morton explored the Chiriquin country, examining a railroad route across the Central American isthmus. In charge of the work on the Washington aqueduct, he was later the superintendent of the construction of Fort Jefferson in the Dry Tortugas (which was later to become the prison for Lincoln conspirators Dr. Samuel Mudd, Michael O'Laughlin, Samuel Arnold, and Edward Spangler).

Morton became the Chief Engineer of the Army of the Ohio in May 1862. He also served in the same capacity with the Army of the Cumberland and was in command of the Pioneer Brigade under General William S. Rosecrans. On April 4, 1863, he was promoted to brigadier general, US Volunteers, to date from the previous November.

Morton reverted to major, Corps of Engineers, in the U.S. Regulars in July 1863, and volunteered to be mustered out of volunteer service in November 1863. During this time he took part in the battles of Stones River and Chickamauga, where he was wounded, as well as breveted for gallantry. Morton also participated in the construction of the defensive works around Chattanooga and Nashville, including Forts Negley and Casino. After this, and until his early 1864 transfer, he supervised the Tennessee garrison.

In January 1864, Morton became the assistant to the Chief Engineer in Washington. The following May he became the Chief Engineer of Major General Ambrose Burnside's Ninth Corps. In this capacity he took part in the Virginia actions at North Anna, Totopotomoy Creek, and Bethesda Church. Morton was killed near Petersburg while reconnoitering ground in preparation for an attack on June 17, 1864.

Morton was posthumously promoted to brigadier general to date from June 17, 1864. During his career he published a number of works including: *An Essay on Instruction in Engineering* (1856), *An Essay on a New System of Fortifications* (1857), *Memoir on Fortification* (1858), *Dangers and Defenses of New York City* (1859), and *Life of Maj. John Saunders of the Engineers.* (1860). (BAM)

Cemetery Location: Section G, Lot 179.

Inscription:

> Brevt Brig. General
> James St. Clair Morton U.S.A.
> of the Engineer Corps
> Promoted for gallant and
> Meritorious Services at
> Stone-River
> Chickamauga
> Petersburg
> Born Sept. 24, 1829
> Killed in Action
> June 17, 1864
>
> *Semper fidelis*

Sources:
Appleton's Cyclopedia of American Biography (7 vols.). New York. 1898.
Faust, Patricia L. *Historical Times Illustrated Encyclopedia of the Civil War.* New York. 1986.
Warner, Ezra. *Generals in Blue: Lives of the Union Commanders.* Baton Rouge. 1964.

Henry Morris Naglee was born in Philadelphia on January 15, 1815. He attended the U.S. Military Academy, graduating in 1835, twenty-third in a class of fifty-six. He was assigned to the 5th Infantry, but resigned after five months to pursue a career as a civil engineer in New York state.

At the outbreak of the Mexican War, Naglee returned to the military and on August 15, 1846, became a captain in the 1st New York Volunteers. After the war he lived in San Francisco where he worked in the banking business until the outbreak of the Civil War.

On May 14, 1861, Naglee was assigned as lieutenant colonel of the 16th U. S. Infantry. He never joined the regiment and resigned on January 10, 1862, however, he was reappointed as a brigadier general on February 12, 1862. He first served in the defenses of Washington, then as a brigade commander in Brigadier General Erasmus D. Keyes's Fourth Corps, Army of the Potomac. During the Peninsula Campaign he was wounded during the battle of Fair Oaks.

Naglee later served in the departments of North and South Carolina, and Virginia and North Carolina. During this time he commanded parts of the Seventh and Eighteenth Corps. During the summer of 1863, Naglee commanded the District of Virginia, where he had a significant disagreement with Governor Francis H. Pierpont of the "Restored Government of Virginia." Naglee refused to support the Governor's demand that the property of persons unwilling to take the oath of allegiance to the United States, as well as the restored government, be forfeited and confiscated. Naglee was relieved of command and ordered to Cincinnati to await orders. When the orders never came, he was honorably discharged from the service on April 4, 1864.

Naglee returned to San Francisco and once again took up the banking profession. In his later years he became interested in the growing of grapes and began a fifty acre vineyard in San Jose. Cultivating Resiling and Charbonneau grapes, he produced a Naglee brandy. On March 5 (?), 1886, while on a visit to his doctor, Naglee died at the Occidental Hotel in San Francisco. (BAM)

Cemetery Location: Section 1, Lots 147/150.

Inscription:

Marie Antoinette
Briggold
Wife of
Gen. Henry M. Naglee
Born Jan 11, 1840
Died May 18, 1869
Gen. Henry M. Naglee
Born Jan. 14, 1816
Died March 6, 1886

Sources:
Appleton's Cyclopedia of American Biography (7 vols.). New York. 1898.
Warner, Ezra. *Generals in Blue: Lives of the Union Commanders.* Baton Rouge. 1964.

Joshua Thomas Owen was born in Caermarthen, Wales, on March 29, 1821. "Paddy," as he was nicknamed, was brought to the United States in 1830, and settled in Baltimore, Maryland. He graduated from Jefferson Academy in Canonsburg, Pennsylvania, in 1845 and was soon admitted to the bar. Along with his brother Robert, Owen founded the Chestnut Hill Academy for boys and taught there for a time. He also practiced law, and from 1857 to 1859 was a member of the Pennsylvania legislature. During this time be joined the militia as a private in the First City Troop of Philadelphia.

At the outbreak of the Civil War, Owen was elected the colonel of the 24th Pennsylvania (May 8, 1861), a ninety-day regiment which remained on the Potomac River during the First Bull Run Campaign. When the 24th was mustered out of federal service, Owen became the colonel of the 69th Pennsylvania and thereafter served in every battle of the Army of the Potomac from Fair Oaks, in the Peninsula Campaign, to Cold Harbor, during the Overland Campaign of 1864. On November 29, 1862, he was promoted to brigadier general for "gallant and meritorious conduct" at the battle of Glendale (June 30, 1862). Although his appointment expired on March 4, 1863, he was renamed on March 30.

During the Overland Campaign, Owen was placed under arrest by his commander, Brigadier General John Gibbon. The charges indicated that on May 18, 1864, near Spotsylvania Court House, Virginia, Owen did not move his brigade up in support of an attacking line, rather he chose to fall back to a line of rifle pits in his rear. Again on June 2, 1864, Owen was charged for failing to mass his men for an attack on June 3 and on that day for failing to properly deploy his men. Despite the charges, he was honorably mustered out of service on July 18, 1864, ending the affair.

Owen returned to Philadelphia and resumed his law practice. In 1866, he was elected the Recorder of Deeds and remained in that position until 1871. During that year he founded the *New York Daily Register*, a law journal which became the official journal of the New York courts until 1873. Owen remained a member of the journal's editorial staff until his death in Chestnut Hill on November 7, 1887. (BAM)

Sources:
Appleton's Cyclopedia of American Biography (7 vols.). New York. 1898.
Warner, Ezra. *Generals in Blue: Lives of the Union Commanders*. Baton Rouge. 1964.

Cemetery Location: Section 5, Lot 81.

Inscription:
Joshua T. Owen
1821-1887

William Painter was born on December 25, 1838, in West Chester, Pennsylvania, the third son of Samuel Marshall and Anne Vickers Painter. He studied at Fort Edward, New York, and at the outbreak of the war, while in Chicago, Painter was one of the first volunteers to enlist in the Sturgis Rifle Corps. The unit was ordered to western Virginia where it served under General George McClellan in a number of actions.

When McClellan was transferred to Washington, he brought the Rifle Corps with him, and Painter was made a lieutenant in the Pennsylvania Reserves.

He was promoted to captain in the Quartermaster's Corps and ordered to duty with General E. O. C. Ord. At the battle of Dranesville (December 20, 1861), Painter's horse was shot out from under him. His gallant behavior, and that of some of his fellow officers, was noted in General Ord's report, which indicated that they should be promoted.

Painter was promoted to major and aide-de-camp on the staff of General James B. Ricketts, and later became the chief quartermaster of the Army of the Potomac's First Corps with the rank of colonel. He participated in actions near Catlett's Station during the Second Manassas Campaign, and was on the staff of Major General John Reynolds at the battle of Gettysburg. Painter was later placed in charge of the transportation of the Army of the Potomac. He was brevetted brigadier general on March 13, 1865, for "faithful and meritorious services."

After the war, Painter engaged in the banking business, and for a time became a member of the Philadelphia Stock Exchange. He eventually devoted himself to the construction of the New York, Philadelphia, and Norfolk Railroad, of which he became vice-president. In 1865 he married Sarah Brown and they had one son. His brother, Uriah, was a war correspondent with the Philadelphia *Inquirer*. General Painter died in Philadelphia on May 3, 1884. (BAM)

Cemetery Location: Section T, Lot 125.

Inscription:
William Painter
Born December 25, 1838
Died May 3, 1884

Sources:
Hunt, Roger D., and Jack R. Brown. *Brevet Brigadier Generals in Blue*. Gaithersburg. 1990.
Painter, Orrin C. *Genealogical and Biographical Sketches of the Family of Samuel Painter*. Baltimore. 1903.

Francis Engle Patterson was born in Philadelphia, on May 7, 1821. Participating in the Mexican War, he entered the military as a second lieutenant in the 1st U.S. Artillery. Promoted to first lieutenant, he remained in the army and was again promoted to captain of the 9th Infantry in 1855. On May 1, 1857, he resigned his commission to return to civilian life concentrating on commercial pursuits.

At the outbreak of the Civil War, Patterson returned to the army as colonel of the 17th Pennsylvania, a ninety-day militia regiment. After duty along the Potomac River, the regiment was detailed to General Robert Patterson's (his father) forces near Martinsburg, Virginia. The regiment was mustered out of service on August 2, 1861. On April 15, 1862, Patterson was promoted to brigadier general and later commanded the Third Brigade of Hooker's Division in Heintzelman's Third Corps serving at Williamsburg and Seven Pines.

In November, Patterson was commanding his own brigade in Hooker's Division under General Daniel Sickles, located at Catlett's Station. During this time, Sickles accused Patterson of an unauthorized retreat in the presence of Confederate forces. Sickles further suggested that Patterson be relieved of command and that an inquiry should be ordered into his conduct. The charges became inconsequential when Patterson was found dead in his tent on November 22, "killed by the accidental discharge of his own weapon." His death occurred at, or near, Fairfax Court House, Virginia. In addition to his father Robert, his brother, Robert Emmet, also attained the rank of general (brevet) during the war. (BAM)

Cemetery Location: Section K, Lots 38-51.

Inscription:

In Memory of
General Francis Engle Patterson
Born May 7, 1821
Died November 22, 1862

A man
true in every relation of life
beloved by his relatives and friends

A soldier
sagacious in [?] intrepid in action
idolized by his officers and men

Sources:
Warner, Ezra. *Generals in Blue: Lives of the Union Commanders*. Baton Rouge. 1964.

Robert Patterson was born in Cappagh, County Tyrone, Ireland, on January 12, 1792. Because of his involvement in the Irish Rebellion of 1798, Robert's father had to escape to the United States. Taking his family, he settled in Delaware County, Pennsylvania. Robert was educated in local schools and eventually became a clerk in a Philadelphia accounting house. Serving in the Pennsylvania militia during the War of 1812, he was commissioned a first lieutenant of infantry. He later served on the staff of General Joseph Bloomfield, remaining in the Regular Army until 1815.

Returning to civilian life, he engaged in manufacturing and established several mills. He became interested in politics and was part of the Pennsylvania convention that nominated Andrew Jackson for president. In 1836, he was the president of the electoral college that cast the Pennsylvania vote for Martin Van Buren. In 1838, and in 1844, he participated in quelling local riots.

At the beginning of the Mexican War, he was appointed major general. He commanded a division at Cerro Gordo, led the advance units in the pursuit of the Mexicans, later entering and capturing Jalapa. After the war he returned to his business ventures and later became the commander of the Pennsylvania Militia.

At the beginning of the Civil War, Patterson was the oldest major general, by commission, in the United States service. On President Abraham Lincoln's initial call for 75,000 three month volunteers, Patterson was mustered into service and assigned to the military departments composing Pennsylvania, Delaware, Maryland, and the District of Columbia.

During Major General Irvin McDowell's advance from Washington in July 1861, Patterson was instructed to prevent General Joseph E. Johnston's Confederate

troops at Winchester from reinforcing General P.G.T. Beauregard at Manassas. Patterson failed to carry out this task which, as he explained, was caused by his failure to receive orders. Highly criticized for his actions he was mustered out of the army at the expiration of his commission on July 27, 1861.

Returning to civilian life, Patterson became one of the largest mill owners in the United States. He was a popular speaker and became the president of the board of trustees of Lafayette College. In 1865 he published *A Narrative of the Campaign in the Shenandoah in 1861*. His sons, Robert Emmet Patterson and Francis Engle Patterson, both became generals during the Civil War. Robert Patterson died in Philadelphia on August 7, 1881. (BAM)

Cemetery Location: Section K, Lot 38.

Inscription:
1812   1846
1861
ROBERT PATTERSON

Sources:
Appleton's Cyclopedia of American Biography (7 vols.). New York. 1898.
Hunt, Roger D., and Jack R. Brown. *Brevet Brigadier Generals in Blue*. Gaithersburg. 1990.

Robert Emmet Patterson, the son of General Robert Patterson, was born on September 8, 1830, at the "Patterson Mansion" on Locust Street in Philadelphia; the present site of the Pennsylvania Historical Society. He attended Georgetown University and entered the U.S. Military Academy on July 1, 1846, graduating in 1851, twenty-ninth in a class

of forty-two. He then assumed the rank of brevet second lieutenant in the 6th U.S. Infantry. He served on the frontier at Ft. Scott, Kansas, and after a sick leave in 1852-54, was at Ft. Ridgely, Minnesota. Patterson became a second lieutenant on January 27, 1853, transferred to Jefferson Barracks, and was part of the 1855 Sioux Expedition where he was in the action at Blue Water (September 3, 1855). Promoted to first lieutenant on September 16, 1856, he was in the Dakota Territory and participated in quelling the Kansas disturbances of 1856. Patterson resigned and was honorably discharged on May 1, 1857.

Patterson was appointed lieutenant colonel and Division Inspector General of the Pennsylvania Militia on April 16, 1861, and was honorably mustered out on June 14, 1861. At this time he became major and Additional Paymaster of U.S. Volunteers. From June to December 1862, he was the colonel of the 115th Pennsylvania Infantry which he aided in recruiting during the spring. The regiment joined the Army of the Potomac at

Harrison's Landing, and after the Peninsula Campaign was assigned to Francis E. Patterson's (his brother) Brigade. He temporarily commanded the brigade in August 1862, but was sick during the battle of Second Manassas. In November 1862, he was ordered to Philadelphia for recruiting services. He resigned his position as colonel on December 2, 1862, and as paymaster on December 23, 1862. On March 13, 1865, he was appointed brevet brigadier general for "meritorious services during the Rebellion."

After the war, Patterson resumed the profession of cotton commission merchant and wool manufacturer. He died in Winnetka, Illinois, on July 14, 1906, leaving a wife and three children. (BAM)

Cemetery Location: Section K, Lot 38.

Inscription:
Robert Emmet Patterson
Bvt. Brig Gen'l U.S.V.
Born Sept. 8, 1830
Died July 14, 1906

Sources:
Annual Reunion, Association of the Graduates of the USMA. 1907.
Hunt, Roger D., and Jack R. Brown. *Brevet Brigadier Generals in Blue.* Gaithersburg. 1990.
Obituary Circular, PA, MOLLUS, Civil War Library & Museum, Philadelphia, PA.

John Clifford Pemberton was born in Philadelphia on August 10, 1814. After entering the United States Military Academy, he graduated twenty-seventh in the fifty-member class of 1837. Assigned to the 4th U.S. Artillery he first served against the Indians in Florida (1837-39)

and along the northern frontier during the Canada border disturbances (1840-42). Pemberton was promoted to first lieutenant on March 19, 1842, and served on garrison duty. He participated in the Mexican War on the staff of General Worth, being breveted captain for gallantry at Monterey and then major for services at Molino del Rey. He was among other Pennsylvania officers thanked by a resolution of the Pennsylvania legislature and received a sword presented by the citizens of Philadelphia. Promoted to captain on September 16, 1850, Pemberton participated in operations against the Seminole Indians, served at Fort Leavenworth, and in the Utah expedition of 1858.

At the outbreak of the Civil War, Pemberton cast his lot with the South, resigning his U.S. Army commission on April 24, 1861. His 1848 marriage to Martha Thompson of Norfolk, Virginia, may have contributed to his decision. He was initially involved with Virginia state troops but was appointed to command the department that included South Carolina, Georgia, and Florida. He was made a brigadier general on June 17, 1861, promoted to major general on January 14, 1862, and lieutenant general on October 10, 1862. Pemberton was appointed to the command of the Department of Mississippi and Eastern Louisiana. Headquartered at Jackson, Mississippi, the department held the important river city of Vicksburg. Conflicting orders from his superiors, General Joseph Johnston and President Jefferson Davis, hampered his ability to perform his duties. He was forced to surrender Vicksburg and its 29,000 soldiers on July 4, 1863, to General U.S. Grant. Returning to Richmond, he remained there until exchanged. As there existed no command which was commensurate with his rank, he resigned and accepted an appointment as a colonel of artillery. Diligent and efficient, he served well in this capacity until the end of the war.

At the end of the Civil War Pemberton retired to a farm near Warrenton, Virginia. In 1876 he returned to Philadelphia where his brothers and sisters lived. In 1881 his health began to fail so he moved to Penlyn, near Philadelphia, where he died on July 13, 1881. (BAM)

Cemetery Location: Section 9, Lot 53

Inscription:
PEMBERTON
JOHN CLIFFORD
August 10, 1814
July 13, 1881
and his wife
MARTHA THOMPSON
May 17, 1827
August 14, 1907

Bronze Plaque:
>JOHN C. PEMBERTON
>Lt. General Staff
>Confederate States Army
>August 10, 1814   July 13, 1881

Sources:
Appleton's Cyclopedia of American Biography (7 vols). New York. 1898.
Warner, Ezra. *Generals in Gray: Lives of the Confederate Commanders*. Baton Rouge. 1864.

Garrett J. Pendergrast, a veteran naval officer, was born in Kentucky on December 5, 1802, and was commissioned a midshipman from that state on January 1, 1812 (at the age of nine!). He was promoted to lieutenant in 1821 and commander on September 8, 1841. At the opening of the Mexican War in 1846, he was in command of the 20-gun sloop *Boston*. Later in the war he was placed in charge of the Navy Yard in Memphis, Tennessee.

Promoted to captain in 1855, the beginning of the Civil War found Pendergrast in command of the Navy's Home Squadron. His flag ship was the 44-gun *Cumberland*. On April 30, 1861, he delivered a notice of blockade to the Confederate officials at Hampton Roads (Norfolk, Virginia area), the first point actually blockaded under President Lincoln's proclamation of April 27.

Promoted to commodore (on the retired list) on July 16, 1862, he was assigned as commandant of the Philadelphia Navy Yard, holding that position until his death from a paralytic stroke on November 7, 1862. His funeral was held at his home on the southwest corner of 12th and Walnut Street's on Monday, November 10. Accompanied by the Marine band, the

procession went to St. Stephen's Episcopal Church on 10th Street for services. His body was temporarily placed in the church vault.

The Philadelphia *Inquirer* described him; "As an officer, Commodore Pendergrast was talented and efficient, and as a man, honorable and respected." (PEP)

Cemetery Location: Section 1, Lot 106.

Inscription:
GARRET J. PENDERGRAST
COMMODORE IN THE U.S. NAVY
BORN IN KENTUCKY DEC 5 1802
DIED IN COMMAND AT THE
NAVY YARD AT PHILADELPHIA
NOV 7 1862

DISTINGUISHED BY [unreadable]
[unreadable]
DUTY AND [unreadable]
[unreadable]
FATHER (?) TO HIS MEN

THE LORD KNOWETH THE DAYS
ON THE [unreadable]
AND THEIR INHERITANCE SHALL
BE [unreadable]

Sources:
Philadelphia *Inquirer*, November 8 & 11, 1862.
Register of the Commissioned, Warrant, and Volunteer Officers of the Navy of the United States. Washington, D.C. Various years.
Spears, John R. *The History of Our Navy From Its Origin to the Present Day, 1775-1897.* New York. 1897.

Charles Mallet Prevost was born in Baltimore, Maryland, on September 19,

1818. After studying law he was admitted to the bar and served as a U.S. Marshal in the Wisconsin Territory. Moving to Philadelphia, he became the deputy collector of the city's port. Active in the local militia, at the outbreak of the Civil War, Prevost was in command of the 1st Regiment, Gray Reserves.

Prevost received an appointment as Assistant Adjutant General to fellow Philadelphian, Brigadier General Francis E. Patterson. After serving in the Peninsula Campaign, he was appointed colonel of the 118th Pennsylvania Infantry (the Corn Exchange Regiment). During the action at Shepherdstown, Virginia (later West Virginia), following the battle of Antietam, the regiment was forced to fall back across the Potomac River, with heavy losses. Seizing the regimental colors, Colonel Prevost ran to the front and rallied his men. While urging them on, he was hit by a minie ball and shell fragment, receiving wounds from which he would never fully recover.

After a partial recovery, Prevost returned to his regiment and participated in the battle of Chancellorsville, with his arm strapped to his body. Following the battle, he was transferred to the Veteran Reserve camp in Harrisburg, Pennsylvania, as colonel of the 16th Regiment. For his actions at Shepherdstown, Prevost was breveted brigadier general on March 13, 1865.

Following the war, Prevost was appointed major general of the Pennsylvania National Guard. He worked for a time as an insurance agent and died in Philadelphia on November 5, 1887. (BAM)

Cemetery Location: Section B, Lot 64.

Inscription:

Caroline S. [unreadable]
wife of
Charles M. Pr [unreadable]
Died Jan. [unreadable]
Charles Mall [unreadable]
[rest of inscription unreadable]

Sources:

Appleton's Cyclopedia of American Biography (7 vols). New York. 1898.
Hunt, Roger D., and Jack R. Brown. *Brevet Brigadier Generals in Blue*. Gaithersburg. 1990.
Smith, John L. *Antietam to Appomattox with the One Hundred and Eighteenth Pennsylvania Volunteers, Corn Exchange Regiment, With Descriptions of Marches, Battles, and Skirmishes, Together with a Complete Roster and Sketches of Officers and Men, Compiled from Official Reports, Letters, and Diaries Profusely Illustrated with Addenda*. Philadelphia. 1892.

William Redwood Price was born in Cincinnati, Ohio, on May 20, 1836, the eighth child of William and Hanna Fisher. He remained there until he was fifteen when he attended school in Pennsylvania, becoming a civil engineer. After working on railroads in that state, Price moved to Chicago where he was a civil engineer on the Galena & Chicago Union Railroad.

At the outbreak of the Civil War, Price was mustered into service as a second lieutenant in the 3rd Pennsylvania Cavalry. He participated in the battle of Williamsburg and the Peninsula Campaign. After the battle of Second

Manassas, Price was promoted to first lieutenant on September 7. He then took part in the battle of Antietam and in various reconnaissances during the winter of 1862-1863. He was promoted to captain on May 1, 1863, and participated in the battle of Chancellorsville before

being assigned to duty as an ordnance officer with the cavalry corps of the Army of the Potomac. After Gettysburg, he was transferred to Washington where he supervised the mounting and equipping of dismounted men. Price was later detailed as ordnance officer and Inspector of Cavalry where he adopted measures to have each regiment uniformly armed.

Price inspected the cavalry in the Western Theater where he found only 9,000 mounted men out of 37,000 present for duty. Returning to the East he was placed in charge of the Cavalry Bureau under the direction of General Henry Halleck. He was promoted to major and Assistant Adjutant General of Volunteers on August 5, 1865, and then brevetted lieutenant colonel of Volunteers on January 23, 1865, for "industry, zeal, and faithful services during the Campaign before Richmond, Va."

Price joined the staff of General Philip Sheridan in February 1865, and participated in the battles of Five Forks, Jettersville, Saylor's Creek, and the surrender of the Army of Northern Virginia at Appomattox Court House. He was breveted brigadier general on March 13, 1865, for "faithful and meritorious services during the war."

At the end of the war, Price accompanied Sheridan to Texas. He participated in engagements with Indians in the West, including Walker's Springs in the Aquarious Range, Arizona, December 10 & 13, 1868. Price died in Germantown, Pennsylvania, on December 30, 1881. (BAM)

Cemetery Location: Section I, Lot 5.

Inscription:

Wm. Redwood Price
Lt. Col. 6th U.S. Cavalry
1836-1881.

Sources:
Appointment, Commission, and Personal Files, National Archives. Washington, DC.
Hunt, Roger D., and Jack R. Brown. *Brevet Brigadier Generals in Blue*. Gaithersburg. 1990.
Regimental History Committee. *History of the Third Pennsylvania Cavalry*. Philadelphia. 1905.

George Campbell Read was born in Ireland around 1787. He came to the United States and became a midshipman on April 2, 1804. Promoted to lieutenant in 1810, he was 3rd lieutenant on the *Constitution* when it captured the British frigate *Guerriére*. Captain Isaac Hull (who is also buried in Laurel Hill Cemetery) honored Read by assigning him to receive the surrender of the British commander. By the end of the War of 1812, Read commanded the *Chippewa* in the squadron commanded by Commodore Oliver H. Perry. He was instrumental in the founding of the Naval Academy and served as the president of the Examination Board which approved the Academy's establishment.

Read was promoted to commander in April 1816, captain in March 1825, and took charge of the East India Squadron in 1840. He later commanded the squadron on the coast of Africa in 1846 and then the Mediterranean squadron. Placed on the reserve list in September 1855, Read was appointed governor of the Naval Asylum in Philadelphia in 1861. He was made rear admiral on the retired list on July 31, 1862, and died on August 22, 1862. Read was initially buried at the Naval Asylum but was later disinterred and moved to Laurel Hill. (BAM)

Cemetery Location: Section 14, Lot 136.

Inscription:
[unreadable]
REAR ADMIRAL GEORGE
CAMPBELL READ
[obliterated]

Sources:
Appleton's Cyclopedia of American Biography (7 vols.). New York. 1891.
Cougar, William B. *Dictionary of Admirals of the U. S. Navy, Volume 1, 1862-1900*. Annapolis. 1989.

Joseph Roberts was born in Middletown, Delaware, December 30, 1814. He attended the University of Pennsylvania and then the U.S. Military Academy, graduating in 1835, eighth in a class of fifty-six. Assigned to the 4th U.S. Artillery, he served in Florida during 1836-1837, leading a regiment of mounted Creek volunteers. From 1837 until 1849, he was an assistant professor of natural and experimental philosophy at his alma mater.

Roberts was promoted to first lieutenant on July 7, 1848, and captain on August 20, 1848. From 1850 to 1858, he participated in the hostilities against the Seminoles in Florida. He then served on frontier duty in Texas, Kansas, and Nebraska. In 1859, he was assigned to Fortress Monroe where he was attached to the artillery school for practice and where he served as a member of the board to arrange the program of instruction. In 1860 Roberts authored the *Hand-Book of Artillery*.

On September 3, 1861, Roberts was promoted to major, and on September 19, 1862, he became the chief of artillery for the Seventh Corps. He received a promotion to colonel of the 3rd Pennsylvania Heavy Artillery on March 19, 1863, and lieutenant colonel of the 4th U.S. Artillery on August 11, 1863.

Colonel Roberts commanded Fortress Monroe from 1863 to 1865, and Fort McHenry, Baltimore, Maryland, in 1865-1866. On March 1, 1865, he was again promoted, this time to brevet brigadier general USA for "meritorious and distinguished services during the war." On April 9, 1865, he was given the rank of brevet brigadier general of Volunteers for "meritorious and distinguished services." He was mustered out of service in November 1865.

Remaining in the Regular Army, Roberts was acting inspector general of the Department of Washington during 1867-1868. He was then made the Superintendent of Theoretical Instruction in the artillery school at Fortress Monroe. He served in this capacity until February

13, 1877. Receiving promotions to colonel, he was placed on the retired list on July 2, 1877, and died in Philadelphia on October 18, 1898. (BAM)

Cemetery Location: Section 3, Lot 41.

Inscription:
> Gen Joseph Roberts
> Born Dec. 30 1814
> Died Oct [?] 1898
> Blessed are the dead who die in the Lord.

Sources:
Appleton's Cyclopedia of American Biography (7 vols.). New York. 1898.
Hunt, Roger D., and Jack R. Brown. *Brevet Brigadier Generals in Blue.* Gaithersburg. 1990.

Richard Henry Rush was born in England on January 14, 1825. He was the son of Richard Rush, the minister to the Court of St. James at the time. He graduated from the Military Academy at West Point in 1846, twenty-sixth in a class of fifty-nine, and became a first lieutenant in the artillery. He served with the regiment and as an instructor at West Point until the beginning of the Mexican War, in which he served with great distinction.

At the beginning of the Civil War, Rush was largely responsible for raising the 6th Pennsylvania Cavalry that was composed of the social, military, and athletic elite of Philadelphia. Rush was made colonel of this unique regiment which used as its primary weapon a 9-foot-long lance with an 11-inch, 3-edged blade, with a scarlet swallow-tailed pennant attached. It was not until 1863 that these weapons were discarded and replaced by carbines. The regiment became widely known as "Rush's Lancers," of whom McClellan commented:

"They are the eyes and ears of my army." Serving with the Army of the Potomac, the regiment participated in many of the battles in the Eastern Theater. Its most memorable action was at Brandy Station (June 9, 1863) where in two determined charges against General JEB Stuart's Confederates they suffered dozens of casualties. Colonel Rush was promoted to brigade command under General Alfred Pleasonton in 1863.

Colonel Rush was recommended for promotion to brigadier general three times. Unfortunately, due to apparent official jealousies, the recommendations were never acted upon. After the war he returned to private life. He died on October 17, 1893, leaving a wife and six children. (BAM)

Inscription:
BORN JAN 14. 1825
DIED OCT. 17. 1893
A LIEUTENANT OF 2ND REGT. U.S. ARTILLERY
IN MEXICAN WAR 1847-48
COL OF 6TH REGT. PENN. CAVALRY LANCERS
IN WAR OF THE REBELLION 1861-1864
SUSAN B RUSH
WIFE OF COLONEL RICHARD HENRY RUSH
BORN APRIL 28. 1828
DIED FEB. 21. 1889

Sources:
Rush File. Cemetery Records. Laurel Hill Cemetery. Philadelphia, PA.

Cemetery Location: Section P, Lots 37 & 40.

Charles Furgeson Smith was born in Philadelphia on April 24, 1807, the son of Dr. William Smith, an army surgeon. In 1821, at the age of fourteen, he was appointed to the Military Academy, graduating in 1825, nineteenth in a class of thirty-seven. He served for many years at the Academy as an instructor, adjutant,

51

and later commandant of cadets. He had a profound influence on a generation of cadets who later became senior commanders in the Union and Confederate armies.

Under the orders of General Zackary Taylor, Captain Smith led four companies of infantry across the Arroyo Colorado in Texas on March 20, 1846, leading to the first confrontation with the Mexican Army. During the bitter fighting outside the city of Monterey that September, he led an assault, under heavy fire, through a waist-deep river and up a rugged hill, driving the Mexicans from their position. He received three brevet promotions (major, lieutenant colonel, and colonel), for gallant and meritorious conduct during the war.

After initially working in recruiting service in the early part of the Civil War, Smith was sent to command a division of troops under one of his former cadets, Ulysses S. Grant. At Fort Donelson, Tennessee, on February 15, 1862, Grant found Smith calmly waiting for orders: "General Smith, all has failed on our right, you must take Fort Donelson." "I will do it," replied Smith, and personally led a bayonet attack that took the outer works without firing a shot. The Confederates surrendered the following day.

Smith was advanced to major general on March 22, 1862, and placed in command of the army advancing up the Tennessee River. Grant resumed command after Smith was injured in an accident. As Sherman reported, "General Smith was quite unwell, and was suffering from his leg, which was swollen and quite sore, from a mere abrasion in stepping into a small-boat. This actually mortified, and resulted in his death about a month later, viz, April 25, 1862."

General Smith's body was returned to Philadelphia on May 3, and was moved to Independence Hall, where it lay in state until Tuesday, May 6. All flags in the city were flown at half mast. At 2:30 p.m. that day, the coffin was carried from Independence Hall and placed in a hearse drawn by six black horses. Three bands and numerous military units were in the procession. According to the Philadelphia *Inquirer*, "The number of people lining the sidewalks and streets throughout the route of the procession was immense." At Laurel Hill Cemetery, the committal services were read by Rev. Dr. Duchachet and salutes were fired by infantry and four pieces of artillery to honor a man that the *Inquirer* referred to as "the very model of a soldier and a general" (PEP)

Cemetery Location: Section X, Lots 438/440.

Inscription:
>Charles F. Smith
>Col 3rd US Infantry
>& Major Gen. Vols.
>Born April 24th 1807
>Died at Savannah Tenn.
>April 25th 1862
>and
>Fanny Mactier Smith
>Wife of
>Charles F. Smith
>Born Dec. 24th 1820
>Died May 26th 1866

Sources:
Grant, U.S. *Personal Memoirs of U. S. Grant.* (2 vols.). New York. 1885.
Philadelphia *Inquirer.* Wednesday, May 2, 1862.
Sherman, William T. *Memoirs of William T. Sherman.* (2 vols.). Bloomington. 1957 reprint.
Smith, Justin H. *The War With Mexico.* (2 vols.). New York. 1919.
Warner, Ezra. *Generals in Blue: Lives of the Union Commanders.* Baton Rouge. 1964.

Alfred Sully was born in Philadelphia on May 22, 1820. He was the son of artist Thomas Sully, who painted the well known work of Thomas Jefferson. Graduating from the U.S. Military Academy in 1841, thirty-fourth in a class of fifty-two, Sully became a second lieutenant in the 2nd U.S. Infantry. He served in the Seminole War participating in the attack on Hawe Creek in 1842.

After serving on garrison duty on the Great Lakes, Sully participated in the siege of Vera Cruz during the Mexican War. Transferred to California, he received a promotion to captain and later took part in operations against the Rouge

River Indians in Oregon. In December 1853, while on his way to New York, he was shipwrecked off the California coast and spent six days on a desert island. Sully served in various frontier posts, and after spending a year in Europe, took part in operations against the Cheyennes until the outbreak of the Civil War.

Sully served in northern Missouri and the defenses of Washington before being appointed to colonel of the 1st Minnesota in 1862. He fought in most of the actions during the Peninsula Campaign, rising to brigade command in Sedgwick's Second Corps Division. After leading his regiment at Antietam, Sully was promoted to brigadier general on September 26, 1862. He was in command of the First Brigade, Second Division, Second Corps, Army of the Potomac at the battles of Fredericksburg and Chancellorsville.

Being more esteemed as an Indian fighter, Sully was transferred west in May

1863, and assigned to the District of Dakota. He lead a number of successful expeditions against the Sioux in Minnesota and the Dakotas. He participated in actions at White Stone Hill (September 1863), Tah-kah-ha-kuty (July 1864) and in the Bad Lands (August 1864). During this time he led an unorthodox force of "Galvanized Yankees," captured Confederates who volunteered to serve on the frontier rather than rotting away in prison camps. At one point his records showed a surplus of mules and a shortage of horses. He was able to balance the books by promoting a number of mules to "brevet horses," showing himself to be a resourceful commander.

At the end of the Civil War, Sully reverted to his Regular Army rank of major. It was only a short time, however, before he was advanced to lieutenant colonel of the 3rd Infantry. In December 1873, he became colonel of the 21st Infantry and served in various administrative positions throughout the West. Assigned to the command of Fort Vancouver, Washington, he commanded only intermittently due to his failing health. He died there on April 27, 1879. (BAM)

Cemetery Location: Section A, Lot 41

Inscription:
> Gen. Alfred Sully USA
> Died at Fort Vancouver
> April 27, 1879

Sources:
Appleton's Cyclopedia of American Biography (7 vols). New York. 1898.
O'Neal, Bill. *Fighting Men of the Indian Wars: A Biographical Encyclopedia of the Mountain Men, Soldiers, Cowboys, and Pioneers Who Took Up Arms During America's Westward Expansion*. Stillwater. 1991.
Warner, Ezra. *Generals in Blue: Lives of the Union Commanders*. Baton Rouge. 1964.

Robert Thompson was born in Philadelphia on January 19, 1828. He was the son of a prominent family and received an education in local schools. Thompson served with the local militia as part of the Washington Grays and participated in the riots of 1844. Just prior to the Civil War he raised a militia company known as the "State Guard," which became Company E of the 17th Pennsylvania, under fellow Philadelphian Francis E. Patterson.

Mustered out after three months, Thompson was appointed lieutenant colonel of the 115th Pennsylvania. The regiment's first duty was to transfer Confederate prisoners captured at Winchester, Virginia, to Fort Delaware, located in the Delaware River just off southern New Jersey, then on to Fortress Monroe, Virginia.

Joining the Army of the Potomac, the regiment took part in the engagement at Malvern Hill, then Bristoe Station. At Second Manassas, Thompson commanded the regiment where he was complimented for his courage and gallantry in the face of a bold and defiant foe. At the end of Major General John Pope's campaign, he was forced to leave the service because of illness and a loss of hearing incurred in the line of duty.

Thompson was breveted brigadier general, U. S. Volunteers, on March 13, 1865, for meritorious services during the rebellion. During the remainder of his life he acted as a railroad executive and merchant, dying in Philadelphia on February 13, 1881. (BAM)

Cemetery Location: Section G, Lot 267.

Inscription:
Gen'l Robert Thompson
Born Jan'y 19th. 1828
Died Feb'y 13th. 1881
Elizabeth S. Thompson
wife of
Gen'l Robert Thompson
Died May 22nd 1912

Sources:
Hunt, Roger D., and Jack R. Brown. *Brevet Brigadier Generals in Blue.* Gaithersburg. 1990.
Thompson File. Cemetery Records. Laurel Hill Cemetery. Philadelphia, PA.

Hector Tyndale was born in Philadelphia, March 24, 1821, the son of an Irish immigrant who had become a successful importer of glass and china. He declined an appointment to West Point, at the request of his mother, in order to enter his father's business. Upon his father's death in 1845, Tyndale began his own porcelain and crystal importing firm, achieving a national reputation for expertise in porcelain.

In 1859, a personal appeal was made to Tyndale to escort Mrs. John Brown

through Philadelphia to Charlestown, Virginia (now West Virginia), to visit her condemned abolitionist husband and help her return his body north following his execution. Although not an abolitionist, Tyndale accompanied Mrs. Brown out of a sense of duty and chivalry. In the course of the self-imposed service, he was subjected to insults, threats, and on the morning of the execution, Tyndale was shot at by an unseen assassin. Tyndale furthered his endearment to the Virginia authorities by demanding that the coffin be opened to positively identify Brown's corpse after posthumous threats were made.

At the outbreak of the Civil War Tyndale was in Paris, France, but hurried home and was commissioned major of the 28th Pennsylvania on June 28, 1861, and lieutenant colonel the following April 25. His regiment took part in battles at Front Royal, Cedar Mountain, and Second Manassas. At the battle of Sharpsburg he commanded, with gallantry, a brigade of the Twelfth Corps, where he was wounded twice. Tyndale was made brigadier general on April 9, 1863, and returned to duty in May. He went on to command a brigade of Howard's Eleventh Corps and then the 3rd Division of that Corps, stationed at Shellmound, Tennessee. On May 2, 1864, he was given a leave of absence because of illness. He resigned on August 26, 1864, and was brevetted major general of Volunteers in March 1865, in recognition of his past services.

After the war Tyndale was again one of Philadelphia's prominent merchants, civic leaders, and philanthropists. He died on March 19, 1880, and was buried in Laurel Hill Cemetery. (TEB)

Cemetery Location: Section H, Lots 1 & 2.

Inscription:

Hector Tyndale
Born March 24, 1821
Died March 19, 1880
"Give me light to see and
strength to do my duty."
Major 28 Pennsylvania Volunteers
June 28, 1861
Lt. Col. 20 Pennsylvania Volunteers
April 25, 1862
Brigadier General U.S. Volunteers
November 29, 1862
For resolute courage conspicuous
gallantry, self possession and
judgement at Antietam
Brevet Major General U.S. Volunteers
March 13, 1865
"For gallant and meritorious services
during the war."

Sources:

Boatner, Mark Mayo, III. *The Civil War Dictionary.* New York. 1959.
Warner, Ezra. *Generals in Blue: Lives of the Union Commanders.* Baton Rouge. 1964.

Clark Henry Wells was born in Reading, Pennsylvania, on September 22, 1822. He was appointed a midshipman in 1840, before attending the Naval Academy in Annapolis in 1846, becoming a midshipman there in July of that year. He served on the brig *Somers*, which capsized and sank off Vera Cruz during the Mexican War. He then joined the crew of the *Petrel*, which participated in covering General Winfield Scott's army's landing, and the bombardment of Vera Cruz. In 1846-1847, Wells participated in the expeditions ending in the capture of Tampico and Tuspan. He was promoted to master in March 1855, and then lieutenant in September of that same year. He then served on the frigate *Niagara*, which laid the first Atlantic sub-marine cable in 1857.

At the outbreak of the Civil War, Wells was appointed executive of the steamer *Susquehanna*, where he participated in the capture of Port Royal, South Carolina. He led numerous boat expeditions in the coastal waters of South Carolina, Georgia, and Florida, which included the capture of Fernandina. During the blockade of Charleston, Wells commanded the sloop *Vandalia*, then served on the sloop *Dale* in 1862.

Wells was commissioned lieutenant commander in July 1862, and was the executive of the Philadelphia Navy Yard in 1863. During the later part of 1863 and early 1864, he commanded the steamer *Galena* in the Western Gulf Blockading Squadron. Participating the battle of Mobile, Alabama, Wells's vessel was lashed to the *Onieda*. When a shell took out the *Onieda's* boiler and wounded its commander, Wells took command of both vessels, towing the *Onieda* to safety. Admiral David G. Farragut commended Wells for his actions in his official report. He then went on to serve in the Eastern Gulf Squadron before joining Admiral David Porter's fleet at Hampton Roads, Virginia, where he remained the rest of the war.

Following the Civil War, Wells commanded the steamer *Kansas* on the Brazil station, where he received the thanks of the British government for assisting a stranded British gun-boat and merchantman. In July 1866, he was commissioned a commander, and then a captain on June 19, 1871. In command of the *Shenandoah*, he assisted the *Compt de Verde*, which had broken from her moorings. For this he received the Legion of Honor from President Theirs of France.

Wells was the chief signal officer of the Navy in 1879-1880, was promoted to commodore in 1880, and then rear-admiral in 1884. He was placed on the retired list on September 22, 1884, and died on January 28, 1888. (BAM)

[Editor's note: No photograph of Clark H. Wells has been found]

Cemetery Location: Section M, Lot 22.

Inscription: REAR ADMIRAL
CLARK H. WELLS
U.S. NAVY
DIED JAN. 28TH 1888
AGED 65 YEARS

Sources:
Appleton's *Cyclopedia of American Biography* (7 vols.). New York. 1891.

Langhorne Wister was born at "Belfield" near Germantown, Pennsylvania, on September 20, 1834, the son of William and Sarah Logan (Fisher) Wister. He attended the Germantown Academy until he was eighteen, at which time he began a career in business by taking a job with the Duncannon Iron Company in Perry County, Pennsylvania. Despite his professional success, he chose the military at the outbreak of the Civil War. Wister became a company commander in the First Rifles or "Bucktail" Regiment of the Pennsylvania Reserves (42nd Pennsylvania Volunteers). The regiment saw its first action at the battle of Dranesville, Virginia, December 20, 1861. Transferred to the Army of the Potomac, Wister participated in the Seven Days battles, with his regiment beginning the initial action of the campaign at Mechanicsburg. He was wounded in the ankle at Gaines's Mill, but was able to remain in command. Serving through Malvern Hill, Wister amassed an excellent record for gallantry and efficiency.

Sent home for recruiting duty, Wister was commissioned colonel of the 150th Pennsylvania Infantry [insultingly dubbed the "Bogus" Bucktails] on September 4, 1862. After spending time in the defenses of Washington, Wister and his regiment joined the Army of the Potomac in February 1863, and took part in the battle of Chancellorsville. At Gettysburg, the 150th participated in the action near the McPherson Farm on July 1. When Colonel Roy Stone was wounded, Wister assumed control of the brigade. Wister was later hit by a minie ball, and although seriously wounded in the mouth, he continued to command the brigade in the thick of the fighting.

Wister resigned his commission in February 1864, and returned to the Duncannon Iron Company. On March 13, 1865, he was breveted brigadier general for "distinguished gallantry at the battle of Gettysburg, Pa., also for gallant conduct at the battles of Fredericksburg and Chancellorsville, Va., and for meritorious services during the war." Langhorne Wister died in Germantown on March 19, 1891, in the house in which he was born.

[The 13th Pennsylvania Reserves, which was known as the original Bucktail Regiment, was raised early in the Civil War by Colonel Thomas L. Kane. See Appendix I.] (BAM)

Cemetery Location: Section L, Lots 316-318.

Inscription:
Langhorne Wister
Born Sept. 20, 1834
Died March 19, 1891
Col. 150th PA Volunteers
Brevet Brigadier General
"In thy light shall we see light"

Sources:
Bates, Samuel P. *Martial Deeds of Pennsylvania*. Philadelphia. 1875.
Hunt, Roger D., and Jack R. Brown. *Brevet Brigadier Generals in Blue*. Gaithersburg. 1990.
Obituary Circular, PA, MOLLUS, Civil War Library and Museum, Philadelphia, PA.

Appendix I

Other Period Notables Buried in Laurel Hill Cemetery

Henry Deringer, Jr., was born in Easton, Pennsylvania, in 1786. Though not a participant in the Civil War, one of his inventions had a large impact at the end of the war and, as such, on American History.

Deringer's father was from Germany and came to America prior to the Revolution. Settling in Richmond, he eventually set up a gun shop. In 1806, the family moved to Philadelphia, where they lived on North Front Street, and had a factory on Tamarind Street. In the 1820s, Deringer concentrated on the production of a compact pocket pistol. His efforts produced the classic, large caliber, short-barreled pistol which today, with a change in spelling, bears his name, the *derringer*.

The derringer became very popular, and by the 1850s was carried by men and women, usually concealed in their clothing. The design was widely copied forcing Deringer to go to court to restrain imitators. It was not until after his death that he won the lawsuit he had filed for trademark infringement. Deringer died, a wealthy and respected Philadelphian in 1868, at the age of eighty-one. He is buried in the Shrubbery section of Laurel Hill Cemetery, Lots 10-14. The monument's inscription simply reads: OUR FATHER.

On April 14, 1865, at Ford's Theater in Washington, D.C., John Wilkes Booth used one of Deringer's pistols to mortally wound President Abraham Lincoln.   (BAM)

[Editor's Note: No photograph of Henry Deringer, Jr. was found.]

Sources: Personal research, Rosa and Stewart B. Harkness, Jr., Friends of Laurel Hill Cemetery Newsletter.

Samuel Gibbs French is not buried in Laurel Hill, and he never was. However, the cemetery does contain a cenotaph [see glossary], within the family plot, mentioning French who was a major general in the Confederate Army. General French was born in Gloucester County, New Jersey, on November 22, 1818. He attended the Military Academy at West Point, graduating in 1843. He was wounded during the Mexican War and resigned from the army to run his wife's Mississippi plantation in 1856.

At the outbreak of the Civil War, French decided to fight for his adopted state, becoming a brigadier general in October 1861, and major general on August 31, 1862. He served in both the Eastern and Western Theaters of the war, which included the command of a division in the Army of Tennessee. After the war he became a planter before retiring to Florida where he died on April 20, 1910, at the age of 92. He is buried in Pensacola. The cenotaph (which is actually the marker for John Clark French and family, in a plot owned by Joseph L. Roberts) is located in Section H, Lot 95. (BAM)

Inscription: SAMUEL GIBBS FRENCH
1818-1910
WEST POINT 1839-1843
CAPTAIN US ARMY
MAJOR GENERAL CS ARMY
BURIAL PLACE PENSACOLA FLORIDA

Sources: Warner, Ezra J. *Generals in Gray: Lives of the Confederate Commanders.* Baton Rouge. 1959.

[Editor's Note: Photographs of General French exist but were not available at the time of publication of this volume.]

Louis Antonie Godey was born in New York City on June 6, 1804. He received little formal education, but instead used books and printing offices as his schools. Moving to Philadelphia in the early 1820s, he became a clerk and "scissors editor" for the *Daily Chronicle*. In 1830, Godey, along with the editor of the *Chronicle*, Charles Alexander, began publishing the *Ladies Book*.

The publication later became known as *Godey's Ladies Book* when Alexander gave up his connection with it. As a fashion magazine, *Godey's* became very popular, eventually reaching a circulation of 150,000. The magazine was unusual in that it used color fashion plates, which up until that time was not done. It also contained contributions from some of the Nineteenth Century's best writers, including Oliver Wendell Hoimes, Henry Wadsworth Longfellow, Edgar Allen Poe, Emma Williams, and Harriet Beecher Stowe. *Godey's* was also unusual in that its editor was a woman, Sarah Josepha Hale.

In 1836 Godey began publishing a literary weekly called the *Saturday News*. This paper eventually became the *Saturday Evening Post*. Godey died a very rich man on either

November 28 or 29, 1878, leaving an estate of more than one million dollars. (BAM)

Cemetery Location: Lot 3, Section W, X, Y, Z.

Inscription: Maria G. Godey
wife of
Louis A. Godey
Born June 7, 1810
Died January 1, 1875
Louis A. Godey
Born June 6, 1804
Died November 28, 1878

Sources:
Dictionary of American Biography (10 vols.). New York. 1960 reprint.
Godey File, Laurel Hill Cemetery Files.

Sarah Josepha Buell Hale was born on October 24, 1788, in Newport, New Hampshire. She received her education from her mother, an older brother who had studied at Dartmouth, and eventually her husband, David Hale. When her husband suddenly died in 1822, Mrs. Hale actively took up a literary career. She wrote a small volume of verse, submitted poems to local periodicals, and wrote a novel called *Northwood, A Tale of New England*.

Mrs. Hale's novel caught the eye of Reverend John Lauris Blake, who offered her the editorship of a monthly women's periodical, the *Ladies' Magazine*, in Boston. This was the first significant American magazine for women. Mrs. Hale's contribution was important, in that she wrote much of every issue herself. She became active in various benevolent and patriotic societies and wrote a number of volumes of prose and verse. One of these volumes, *Poems for Our Children*, contained the well-known poem *Mary Had a Little Lamb*.

In 1837, Louis A. Godey bought the *Ladies' Magazine* and made Mrs. Hale the literary editor of the *Lady's Book*. In 1841 she moved to Philadelphia where, under her guidance, *Godey's Ladies Book* became one of the best known American periodicals for women.

Mrs. Hale retired from the magazine in 1877, in her eighty-ninth year. Remaining in Philadelphia, she died on April 30, 1879, and was buried in Laurel Hill, Section X, Lot 61. (BAM)

Sources: *Dictionary of American Biography* (10 vols.). New York. 1960 reprint.

Thomas Leiper Kane, like Samuel Gibbs French, is not buried in Laurel Hill Cemetery. But he was.

Kane was born in Philadelphia on January 27, 1822, and temporarily attended school in Europe. Returning to the United States he studied under his father, a federal judge for the eastern district of Pennsylvania. Tension between the two over slavery eventually caused a split in the family (Kane was an abolitionist while his father supported the Fugitive Slave Law).

Kane served for a time as an agent on the Underground Railroad. He accompanied the Mormons west and in 1858 convinced Brigham Young that it was useless to resist the U. S. Army. Moving back east, just before the outbreak of the Civil War, he founded the town of Kane, Pennsylvania.

At the outbreak of the war he raised the 42nd Pennsylvania Volunteers, better known as the 13th Pennsylvania Reserves or the "Bucktails." Raised from woodsmen and hunters, the regiment was composed of excellent marksmen who wore a buck's tail on their kepi to signify their membership in the regiment.

During the fighting in the Shenandoah in 1862, Kane was wounded twice and captured at Harrisonburg. Later exchanged, he was promoted to brigadier general on September 7, 1862. He served at Antietam, Chancellorsville, and Gettysburg. Resigning from the army for health reasons in November 1863, Kane spent the remainder of his life living in Kane and in Philadelphia. In 1865 he was breveted major general for his services at the battle of Gettysburg.

Kane was the first president of the Pennsylvania state board of charities, a director of a number of business enterprises, and the author of three books. He died in Philadelphia on December 26, 1883, and was buried in Laurel Hill Cemetery. The family vault remains in the Cemetery in an almost inaccesable site overlooking the Schuylkill River, Section P, Lot #100. The inscription simply reads: KANE

In 1884, thanks to the petitioning of the citizens of Kane, the General's body was removed from Laurel Hill and reinterred in the town he founded. (BAM)

Sources: Warner, Ezra. *Generals in Blue: The Lives of the Union Commanders.* Baton Rouge. 1964.

Thomas Buchanan Read The tall, black obelisk facing the Fitler Circle bears the name Thomas Buchanan Read. Every cultivated American of the post-Civil War period knew Read as both a highly regarded painter and a widely acclaimed poet. School children and veterans alike could recite his poem "Sheridan's Ride."

Read was living a cultivated life in the American community in Rome when he first learned of the firing on Fort Sumter. He had come a long way from his rural boyhood near Downingtown in Chester County. He had gained a considerable reputation for paintings as "The Embarkation of Cleopatra" and "Time Rescuing Proserpine." He had won the praise of Longfellow for his collections of poems.

But happy as he was in the artistic community of Rome, Read felt at once that he had to volunteer for the war effort. He returned home and served on the staffs of General Lew Wallace and General William Rosecrans.

Read's purpose was to inspire the nation with speeches and poems. His lyrics and narratives were read by him and famous tragedians in theaters, at public rallies, and in army hospitals. General Grant, Sherman, and Sheridan praised his work. President Lincoln carried a copy of Read's poem "The Oath" in his memorandum book.

An obituary sketch states that "it is well known that in several instances where an apathetic spirit brooded over a community, the thrilling words of Mr. Read woke them from their ignoble repose, rekindled the fire of patriotism, and sent them forth to conquer or die."

Read's best known war poem is "Sheridan's Ride." He wrote the eight stanza poem in Cincinnati after a friend showed him Thomas Nast's dramatic drawing of "Sheridan's Ride to the Front" in a November 1864 issue of Harper's Illustrated Weekly.

His accompanying article explained that the Union General was in Winchester, Virginia, when he learned that the enemy had attacked his troops many miles away at Cedar Creek. The Confederates had the advantage of surprise and appeared to be winning, when the General suddenly arrived on the field riding, said a member of his staff, "so that the devil himself could not have kept up."

Nast's drawing showed the General furiously spurring his horse through the Virginia countryside. "There's a poem in that picture," a friend declared, and asked that it be written in time to be declaimed at a public meeting that very evening. "Do you suppose I can write a poem to order," Read indignantly asked, "just as you would go to Sprague's and order a coat?"

Nevertheless, he called for a cup of strong tea and gave orders that he was not to be disturbed. Within a few hours he had produced a poem of eight stanzas.

In the poem, Read transfers attention from the mind of the anxious General to the effort of his gallant horse. In the fist stanza, "the terrible grumble, and rumble, and roar" tells that "the battle was on once more,/ and Sheridan twenty miles away."

Once the ride is on, Read transfers attention from the thoughts of the worried general to the spirit of his gallant horse. By the end of the third stanza, Sheridan's steed is pounding down the road and "his heart was gay,/ With Sheridan fifteen miles away."

In the next stanza, the horse is zooming like a comet:

> The heart of the steed, and the heart of the master,
> Were beating like prisoners assaulting their walls,
> Impatient to be where the battle-field calls;
> Every nerve of the charger was strained to full play,
> With Sheridan only ten miles away.

Sheridan arrives to find his forces in retreat, but the sight of general and horse bring the fleeing troops to a sudden halt. By nightfall a certain defeat had been transformed into victory.

After the war, Thomas Buchanan Read returned to Rome where he lived with this second wife and served as a guide and host to visiting Americans. His health received a serious shock in the autumn of 1871. The carriage in which Read was taking New Jersey's Governor Ward to the Coliseum pitched into an excavation. Read was knocked unconscious. His health declined rapidly during the winter and he felt a strong desire to return to the United States. He caught pneumonia on the boat and died in New York's Astor House hotel on May 4, (?) 1872.

The funeral took place at the home of Read's brother-in-law on Manheim Street in Germantown. Among his pall bearers were George Childs, publisher of the *Public Ledger* and General Hector Tyndale, both now buried in Laurel Hill Cemetery. (MB)

Inscription: T. Buchanan Read
　　　　　　　　Born
　　　　　　March 12, 1822
　　　　　　　　Died
　　　　　　　May 11, 1872
　　　　　　　His Wife
　　　　　　Harriet Denison
　　　　　　 Aug. 20, 1837
　　　　　　 Dec. 17, 1935

Cemetery Location: Section K. Lot 206.

Sources:
Jackson, Joseph. *Literary Landmarks of Philadelphia.* Philadelphia. 1939.
Townsend, Henry Clay. *A Memoir of Thomas Buchanan Read.* Printed for Private Circulation. Philadelphia. 1889.

William Moffet Reilly was born in Philadelphia on March 13, 1822. He was educated at the academy of Michael Roach in Philadelphia, studied law for a time, and then took up pharmacology as a profession. He later engaged in the real estate business and politics.

He was active in the militia, becoming a lieutenant in the Wayne Artillery. Because the state's quota was full, the unit and Reilly did not serve during the Mexican War. He rose through the militia ranks and eventually reached the rank of brigadier general before taking command of the Third Brigade, Pennsylvania troops.

At the outbreak of the Civil War, Reilly was placed in command of the First Division Pennsylvania Volunteers and Philadelphia troops not in federal service. Meanwhile the Third Brigade marched off to war without him. Reilly's problem appeared to be that he had been elected to his rank rather than appointed. He tried, unsuccessfully, to obtain a command and eventually focused on the care and relief of the wounded and promoting the interests of the soldiers at the front.

Following the war, Reilly was appointed an inspector of county prisoners. Remaining active in politics he was a delegate to the Chicago convention that nominated George McClellan for president.

More than forty years after his death, Reilly's trust accumulated enough money to erect statues of Revolutionary War notables LaFayette, Montgomery, Pulaski, and Steuban. It was originally planned that these statues were to be placed in front of Independence Hall, but today they sit on the West Terrace of the Philadelphia Art Museum, which is called "The Terrace of Heroes: Reilly Memorial." Statues were later added of John Paul Jones (1957) and Nathaniel Greene (1962).

Reilly died on February 29, 1896, and lies in an impressive mausoleum overlooking the Schuylkill River, River Section, Lots 1, 2, 3 & 4. (BAM)

Sources: Personal Research by Stewart B. Harkness, Jr., Laurel Hill Cemetery Newsletter.
Gordon, G. F. Sketch of William M. Reilly.

George Alfred Townsend was born in Delaware on January 30, 1841. He was to become the youngest war correspondent of the Civil War, serving both at home and abroad. He reported for newspapers in Philadelphia, New York, and Washington, signing his work with the pen name "GATH," a variation on his initials inspired by the biblical passage: (II Samuel 1:20) "Tell it not in Bath, publish it not in the streets of Askalon." His work was highly respected. President Lincoln reportedly once commented on whether or not he should visit a battlefield: "No, it is not necessary for me to go there. George Alfred Townsend has been there." During the Reconstruction Era he became one of America's most important journalists.

In 1884, Townsend purchased a tract of land on South Mountain, Maryland, near the site of the 1862 battle of Crampton's Gap. The site, just east of Burkittsville, was an area of fierce fighting between Union and Confederate troops just prior to the battle of Antietam. Here he built a home which he named Gapland Hall. Townsend built a number of buildings on his property but the most striking was a stone arch monument which looks like a one-walled castle. Inscribed on the monument are the names of 157 reporters, newspaper and Army artists, both North and South, who covered the Civil War. The monument was dedicated on October 16, 1896, and later turned over to the War Department for administration.

Townsend covered the assassination of Abraham Lincoln and the pursuit of John Wilkes Booth. In later years he worked on the history of the Delmarva Peninsula, and shortly before his death authored a book "Delaware Poems."

One of the buildings erected near Gapland Hall was a mausoleum which may have been intended a becoming Gath's final resting-place. However, when

he died on April 15, 1914, his remains were brought to Philadelphia. He is buried in the Laurel Hill family plot.

Today, the home and monument he built is a park administered by the state of Maryland. (BAM)

Cemetery Location: Section 9, Lot 98.

Inscription:

GEORGE
ALFRED TOWNSEND
1841-1914
GATH

Sources: George Alfred Townsend by John LaRosch, Laurel Hill Cemetery Newsletter #35, Spring 1993.
Visitors brochure, Gathland State Park.

Appendix II

Medal of Honor Recipients in Laurel Hill Cemetery

Henry H. Bingham (See page 1).

Robert Teleford Clifford (Robert T. Kelly) was born in Pennsylvania in 1835. He entered the United States Navy where he attained the rank of Master's Mate. On December 31, 1864, he was awarded the Medal of Honor. The citation read:

> Served on board the U.S.S. *Shokokon* at New Topsail Inlet off Wilmington, N.C., 22 August 1863. Participating in a strategic plan to destroy an enemy schooner, Clifford aided in the portage of a dinghy across the narrow neck of land separating the sea from the sound. Launching the boat in the sound, the crew approached the enemy from the rear and Clifford gallantly crept into the rebel camp and counted the men who outnumbered his party three to one. Returning to his men, he ordered a charge in which the enemy was routed, leaving behind a schooner and a quantity of supplies.

He died in Philadelphia on July 24, 1873, and was buried in Laurel Hill Cemetery. (BAM)

Cemetery Location: Section 17, Lot 149.

Inscription: ROBERT T. KELLY
DIED JULY 24, 1873
AGED 38 YEARS
LOUISA WIGLEY
WIFE OF
ROBERT T. KELLY
1840-1898
M. G. KELLEY
BORN JANUARY 11, 1870
DIED JANUARY 25, 1870

Bronze Plaque:
ROBERT T. KELLY
MEDAL OF HONOR
MA US NAVY
CIVIL WAR
USS SHOKOKON
1835   1873

Sources: Gerard F. White, Congressional Medal of Honor Society.

Frank Furness was born on November 11, 1839, in Philadelphia. His father, William Henry Furness, was a well-known clergyman and abolitionist. Taking up the profession of architecture, he studied under Richard Morris Hunt, who was considered to be an expert in the field.

The Civil War broke out while Furness was studying in New York, so he joined the federal cavalry. When he was discharged in October 1864, he was a captain in the 6th Pennsylvania Cavalry. In 1899, he petitioned for and received the Medal of Honor for his actions at the battle of Trevilian Station, Virginia, where he voluntarily carried a box of ammunition across an open space swept by enemy fire. Furness is the only American architect of note to have received such an award.

Following the war, Furness returned to Philadelphia where he became a successful architect constructing some 650 buildings, and becoming one of the most highly paid architects of his time. The majority of his work was done between 1870 and 1895, and includes some of Philadelphia's most prominent buildings, including the Philadelphia Zoo Gatehouses, the Pennsylvania Academy of Fine Arts, and the Merion Cricket Club.

By the time of his death in 1912, Furness's work had fallen out of favor and his obituary barely mentioned that he had been an architect. Today, Frank Furness is considered to be the first real "All-American" architect. (BAM)

Cemetery Location: Section S, Lot 94.

Bronze Plaque Inscription:
        FRANK FURNESS
        MEDAL OF HONOR
        CAPT CO F
        6TH PA CAV
        NOV 12 1839
        JUN 27 1912

Sources: Harkness, Rosa. Personal Research. Friends of Laurel Hill Cemetery Newsletter.

George J. Pitman was a sergeant in Company C, 1st New York (Lincoln) Cavalry. At the battle of Saylor's Creek, April 6, 1865, during the retreat of the Army of Northern Virginia towards Appomattox Court House, Sergeant Pitman captured the flag of the Sumter Heavy Artillery. For his actions he was awarded the Medal of Honor which was issued on May 3, 1865. (BAM)

Cemetery Location: Section 3, Lot 32.

Inscription:

IN MEMORY OF
GEORGE J. PITMAN
DIED APRIL 30, 1884
AGED 45 YEARS

Bronze Plaque:

GEORGE J. PITMAN
MEDAL OF HONOR
SERG CO C 1ST NY CAV
CIVIL WAR
1839   1884

Sources:
UGPO. *The Medal of Honor of the United States Army.* Washington. 1948.
Gerard F. White, Congressional Medal of Honor Society.

John Hamilton Reid Storey was born in Philadelphia on April 14, 1836. He received the Medal of Honor for his actions during the fighting at Dallas, Georgia, May 28, 1864. The citation read: "While bringing in a wounded comrade, under a destructive fire, he was himself wounded in the right leg, which was amputated on the same day." The medal was awarded on August 29, 1896.

Storey died in Philadelphia on April 10, 1916. (BAM)

Cemetery Location: Section V, Lot 74.

Inscription:
JOHN H. R. STOREY
1836-1916

Bronze Plaque:
JOHN H. R. STOREY
MEDAL OF HONOR
SERG CO F 109 PA INF
CIVIL WAR
1836   1916

Sources:
UGPO. *The Medal of Honor of the United States Army.* Washington. 1948.
Gerard F. White, Congressional Medal of Honor Society.

Pinkerton Vaughn was born in Downingtown, Pennsylvania, in 1839. During the Civil War he served in the U.S. Marine Corps, and for his actions at the battle of Port Hudson was awarded the Medal of Honor. The citation read:

> Serving on board of the USS *Mississippi* during her abandonment and firing in the action with the Port Hudson batteries, 14 March 1863. During the abandonment of the *Mississippi* which had to be grounded, Sergeant VAUGHN rendered invaluable assistance to his commanding officer, remaining with the ship until all the crew had landed and the ship had been fired to prevent its falling into enemy hands. Persistent until the last, and conspicuously cool under the heavy shellfire, Sergeant VAUGHN was finally ordered to save himself as he saw fit.

Vaughn died on August 22, 1866. (BAM)

Cemetery Location: Section 16. Lots 412-416.

Inscription:

PINKERTON VAUGHN
MEDAL OF HONOR
SERG
USMC
USS MISSISSIPPI
1841
1866

Sources: Pinkerton file. United States Marine Corps, History & Museum Division, Washington, DC.

Appendix III

Some Other Laurel Hill Civil War Burials

Charles Frederick Abbot	33rd Pennsylvania
Captain H. A. Adams	United States Navy
Colonel R. W. Pomeroy Allen	
Major Alexander Biddle	121st Pennsylvania
Captain Henry J. Biddle	Pennsylvania Reserves
Lieutenant William Bowen	75th Pennsylvania
Lieutenant Colonel Charlie Boyd	17th United States
Lieutenant William Howard Brice	United States Navy
Lieutenant Colonel William Brisbane**	49th Pennsylvania
Lieutenant Henry Chancellor	150th Pennsylvania
Antony A. Clay	58th Pennsylvania
Lieutenant Fletcher Clay	145th Pennsylvania
Parker Colladay (buried Bull Run battlefield)	
Major Horace A. Conant	
John D. Cooper	1st New Jersey Cavalry
Robert P. Corson	
Arthur Henry Craige	15th Anderson's Cavalry
Augustus T. Cross.	2nd Pennsylvania Reserves
Lieutenant Colonel A. Boyd Cummings	
Lieutenant Colonel William Lovering Curry	106th Pennsylvania
Colonel Charles Dare	23rd Pennsylvania
Richard Wistar Davids	118th Pennsylvania
Lieutenant Colonel Thomas H. Davis	12th New Jersey
Reverend Edward Kirk Donaldson	23rd New Jersey
Thomas H. Elliott	
Augustus Falsteth	24th Pennsylvania
Lieutenant Colonel Maurice E. Fagen	19th Pennsylvania Cavalry
Lieutenant Caesar Rodney Fisher	1st U.S. Cavalry
Lieutenant Edwin Ford	119th Pennsylvania
William Henry Ford	44th Pennsylvania Surgeon
Lieutenant Frederick Grill	3rd Pennsylvania Artillery
Louis Grill	
Charles B. Grieves.	6th Pennsylvania Heavy Artillery
Lieutenant Evan W. Grubb	15th Anderson's Cavalry
Lieutenant Lorance W. Grugan	
Lieutenant John Hazeltine Haddock	8th Pennsylvania Cavalry
Lieutenant Sam B. Haines	121st Pennsylvania
Lieutenant Colonel William Henry Harrison	214th Pennsylvania
D. Stanley Hassinger	119th Pennsylvania

Corporal William J. Harvey	82nd Pennsylvania
James F. Hollins	
Captain Thomas C. James	9th Pennsylvania Cavalry
William B. Jones	31st Pennsylvania
Lieutenant Arthur Keene	
Robert B. Kerr	
Byron G. Keyser	23rd Pennsylvania
Colonel James W. Latta	
Lieutenant Horace M. Lee	81st Pennsylvania
Captain Henry Lelar, Jr.	
Lieutenant Colonel George F. Leppein	5th Maine
Sergeant Richard Martin	
Lieutenant Clayton McMichael	9th U.S. Infantry
Colonel Gabriel Middleton**	20th Pennsylvania Cavalry
Corporal John Michener	118th Pennsylvania
Elihu Spencer Miller	United States Artillery
Captain William C. Moss	119th Pennsylvania
Major James P Wilson Neill	
Captain Walter S. Newell	3rd Pennsylvania Cavalry
Captain John C. Oberteuffer	1st Mounted Rifles (NY)
Lieutenant Colonel Henry O"Neill	118th Pennsylvania
Reverend William J. O'Neill	118th Pennsylvania
Lieutenant Harry Overman	
Captain Alban T. Paist	71st Pennsylvania
Lieutenant Adolphus W. Peabody	
Chief Philip G. Peltz	
Lieutenant Samuel H. Peltz	USS *America*
Horatio B. Penncock, Jr.	
Major Francis J. Randall	95th Pennsylvania
William Brooke Rawle	3rd Pennsylvania Cavalry
Francis M. Ritchie	72nd Pennsylvania
Emelen Ritter	72nd Pennsylvania
Colonel Harry Rockafellar	71st NYSM
Major Adolph Rosengarten	15th Anderson's Cavalry
Lieutenant Joseph Rosengarten	121st Pennsylvania
Captain William Sargent	12th Pennsylvania, 210th Pennsylvania
Charles J. Shinn	
Thomas T. Shoch	
Captain E. P. Shoenberger	
Captain William Swain Small	26th Pennsylvania
Henry Hollingsworth Smtih	
Warren Supplee	15th Anderson's Cavalry
Major Charles F. Taggart	2nd Pennsylvania Cavalry
Colonel Thomas F. B. Tapper	33rd Pennsylvania

Edward F. Taylor   192nd Pennsylvania
Colonel Lewis F. Taylor   42nd Pennsylvania
John Wesly Thompson   141st Pennsylvania
Dr. Charles S. Turnbull   119th Pennsylvania
Colonel William Clark Ward   17th and 115th Pennsylvania
Captain Raphael Wenas
Captain David Wilcox
Captain Augustus H. D. Williams   5th U.S. Cavalry
Thomas C. Williams   19th U.S. Infantry
William Wirt   39th Illinois
Theodore J. Wright

** The monuments over the graves of these two colonels refer to them as GENERAL. According to Roger D. Hunt, author of *Brevet Brigadier Generals in Blue*, neither Brisbane nor Middleton were awarded a promotion to brevet brigadier or major general. The reason for GENERAL, as of the publication of this book, is lost to history.

This list does not claim to be a complete listing of the Civil War burials in Laurel Hill Cemetery. It is simply a listing of individuals discovered while doing other research.

Appendix IV

Some Other Notables Buried in Laurel Hill

Matthias W. Baldwin: The first person in the United States to develop the steam locomotive and the founder of Baldwin's Locomotive Works.

William Cresson: Following his death in his twenties, Cresson's family established a fellowship in his honor at the Pennsylvania Academy of Fine Arts which is still awarded today.

Henry Disston: Disston immigrated from England and apprenticed to the saw-making trade in the 1830s. He formed his own company that produced high quality saws which, at the time of his death, employed 600 men.

Richard Dale: First lieutenant under John Paul Jones during the engagement between the *Serapis* and the *Bonhomme Richard*, September 1779.

Robley Dunglison: Medical advisor to Presidents Thomas Jefferson and James Madison. He spent much of his career associated with the Jefferson College of Medicine.

Edwin Fitler: Mayor of Philadelphia from 1887-1891. Fitler Square and the Fitler School are named after him.

Adam Forepaugh: Circus owner and rival of P. T. Barnum.

Henry D. Gilpin: Attorney General of the United States and President of the Pennsylvania Academy of Fine Arts.

Thomas Godfrey: Inventer of the Mariner's Quadrant.

Simon Gratz: Philadelphia philanthropist, educator, and politician.

Benjamin Hodgson: Lieutenant Hodgson was a graduate of the Military Academy at West Point who had the misfortune of being attached to the 7th US Cavalry on June 25, 1876. As part of Lt. Colonel George A. Custer's command at the battle of the Little Big Horn, Hodgson was killed during Major Marcus Reno's retreat from the initial attack on the Indian village. Hodgson was one of the few bodies removed from the Custer Battlefield in 1877.

Isaac Hull: Commodore Isaac Hull was the commander of the USS *Constitution* during the War of 1812.

Elijah Kent Kane: Explorer and author of *Arctic Explorations*.

Samuel King: Twelfth mayor of Philadelphia who prohibited fireworks on the 4th of July. He allowed African-American officers on the police force, and advocated a Centennial Exposition.

Henry Charles Lea: Historian and reformer who founded the Union League.

Napoleon Le Brun: Architect of the Academy of Music and the Cathedral of Saints Peter and Paul.

Joshua B. Lippincott: Founder of the Philadelphia publishing company that still bears his name.

John McArthur: Architect of Philadelphia City Hall.

Thomas McKean: McKean was one of the signers of the Declaration of Independence.

Morton McMichael: Journalist and post Civil War mayor of Philadelphia.

Hugh Mercer: A physician who served in Scotland's Battle of Colloden in 1745, Mercer came to America and served under George Washington in the French and Indian War and later in the Revolutionary War. He died at the battle of Princeton and his remains were transferred to Laurel Hill in 1840.

Samuel George Morton: A scientist who led in the development of physical anthropology and who helped develop the Philadelphia Academy of Natural Sciences.

William James Mullen: A poor youngster who made a fortune in manufacturing gold watch dials. Mullen later devoted his life to charity and helping convicts.

John Notman: Architect of Laurel Hill Cemetery.

Boise Penrose: Colorful leader of the Republican Party in Philadelphia in the early 20th Century. Probably best known today for an avenue and bridge in South Philadelphia.

Joseph Reed: Revolutionary War general, aide, and secretary to George Washington.

David Rittenhouse: Skilled clock maker, mathematician, engineer, revolutionary, and world renowned astronomer. In 1763 he surveyed the boundary of Delaware and Pennsylvania which became the cornerstone for the Mason-Dixon Line. Rittenhouse Square in Center City Philadelphia is named after him.

Richard Rush: Minister to England during the administration of President James Madison and known for his treaty negotiations.

William Short. Received the first appointment to public office conferred under the Constitution of the United States.

Thomas Sully: Father of Civil War general Alfred Sully. Sully was an artist who's works include a portrait of Thomas Jefferson and Washington Crossing the Delaware.

Charles Thomson: Thomson was the corresponding secretary of the Continental Congress. Though not originally interred in Laurel Hill, Thomson and his wife Hanna were reinterred there from their original burial ground in Harriton near Bryn Mawr.

Richard Vaux: Pre-Civil War mayor of Philadelphia.

Joseph L. Warton: One of the founders of Swarthmore College and founder of the Warton School of Finance and Political Economy at the University of Pennsylvania.

Peter A. B. Widner: Starting out as a butcher, Widner made a fortune during the Civil War selling meat to the Union army. He later became known for his work with the trolley lines within the city of Philadelphia. At the time of his death he was perhaps the wealthiest man in the city.

Jonathan Williams: Williams was the first superintendent of the U. S. Military Academy at West Point.

Alexander Wilson: Leading American ornithologist.

Owen Wister: Author best known for *The Virginian*.

Jacob Zelin: Brigadier General and Marine Corps Commandant.

Sources:

Michael Brooks. *A Walking Tour at Laurel Hill Cemetery.*
Rosa and Stewart B. Harkness, Jr. *A Driving Tour of Laurel Hill Cemetery.*

Glossary

Brevet Rank (BVT)	Honorary title awarded for gallant or meritorious services during the time of war. Brevet ranks have none of the authority, precedence, or pay of the full rank.
GAR	Grand Army of the Republic. Post-war Union veterans group.
USA	United States Army
USV	United States Volunteers
Cenotaph	Empty tomb. Monument erected in honor of a person or persons who's remains are buried elsewhere. Often used with lives lost at sea.

Tombstone Symbols

Angel	Assists the soul's journey to Heaven.
Book	The open book refers to the Bible or the book of life, which acted as a record of the deeds of the righteous. The names omitted from this book could not enter Heaven.
Column	Draped column signifies mortality. Broken column symbolizes a life cut short.
Cross and Crown	Symbolizes the reward of the faithful Christian after death.
Gun, Sword, Cannon, Anchor	Grave of a soldier or sailor.
Ivy	Immortality.
Lamb	Innocence; often used on a child's grave.
Obelisk	Eternal life; from the Egyptian sun worshipping symbol.
Torch	Down-turned symbolizes life extinguished.
Urn	Draped symbolized death. Shattered indicates violent death.
Wreath	Variation on the crown, symbolizing the victory of life over death.

Sources: Michael Brooks. *A Walking Tour at Laurel Hill Cemetery.*
Rosa and Stewart B. Harkness, Jr. *A Driving Tour of Laurel Hill Cemetery.*
Colleen McDannell. "The Religious Symbolism of Laurel Hill Cemetery." *The Pennsylvania Magazine of History and Biography.* Volume CXI. Number 3. 1987.

Photograph Credits

Civil War Library and Museum
Henry Bohlen, p. 4
Ulric Dahlgren, p. 12
Percival Drayton, p. 14
Sylvanus William Godon, p. 21
Thomas Kane, p. 65
George Meade, Jr., p. 31
James St. Clair Morton, p. 33
John Clifford Pemberton, p. 42
Richard Henry Rush, p. 50
Hector Tyndale, p. 56

Roger D. Hunt Collection
Henry Harrison Bingham, p. 1
George Alexander Hamilton Blake, p. 2
Gideon Clark, p. 5
Louis Raymond Francine, p. 19
Edgar Mantlebert Gregory, p. 22
Caldwell Kepple Hall, p. 23
John William Hoffman, p. 24
William David Lewis, Jr., p. 27
William Redwood Price, p. 47
Joseph Roberts, p. 49
Langhorne Wister, p. 58

Blake A. Magner Collection
George Gordon Meade, p. 28

Massachusetts MOLLUS Collection, United States Army Military History Institute
Thomas Jefferson Cram, p. 6
Samuel Wylie Crawford, p. 7
John Adolph Bernard Dahlgren, p. 10
Oliver Blachy Knowels, p. 25
Henry Morris Neglee, p. 35
Joshua Thomas Owen, p. 36
Francis Engle Patterson, p. 38
Robert Patterson, p. 40
Garrett Pendergrast, p. 44
Charles Mallet Prevost, p. 45
Charles Ferguson Smith, p. 51
Alfred Sully, p. 53
Robert Thompson, p. 54

85

Frederick H. Meserve. *Historical Portraits.* **Courtesy of the New York State Library.**
Benzet Forst Foust, p. 18
William Painter, p. 37

National Archives
Alexander Cummings, p. 8

Roster, Department of Illinois, GAR
Robert Emmet Patterson, p. 41

Charles Ellet, Jr.: *The Engineer as Individualist. 1810-1862.* **by Gene D. Lewis.** © **1968 by the Board of Trustees of the University of Illinois.**
Charles Ellet, Jr., p. 15
Charles Rivers Ellet, p. 16

American Authors 1600-1900: A Biographical Dictionary of American Literature. **Edited by Stanley J. Kunitz and Howard Haycraft. H. W. Wilson Company. 1955 reprint.**
Louis Antonie Godey, p. 63
Sarah Josepha Hale, p. 64
Thomas Buchanan Read, p. 66

Blue & Gray Magazine
George Alfred Townsend, p. 69

Sketch of William M. Reilly, by G. F. Gordon.
William Moffet Reilly, p. 68

Dictionary of Admirals of the U. S. Navy, Volume 1, 1862-1900, **by William B. Cougar, Annapolis. 1989.**
George Campbell Read, p. 48

All cemetery photographs by Blake A. Magner

Index

Antietam, Battle of, 8, 18, 26, 29, 31, 45, 47, 53, 56, 57, 65, 69
Bingham, Henry, 1, 2, 71
Blake, George, 2, 3
Bohlen, William, 3, 4
Chancellorsville, Battle of, 12, 18, 20, 21, 22, 29, 46, 47, 53, 53, 59, 65
Clark, Gideon, 5, 6
Clifford, Robert, 71
Cram, Thomas, 6, 7
Crawford, Samuel, 7, 8
Cummings, Alexander, 8, 9, 10
Dahlgren, John, 10, 11, 12, 13
Dahlgren, Ulric, 12, 13
Deringer, Henry, Jr., 61
Drayton, Percival, 14
Ellet, Charles, Jr., 14, 15, 16
Ellet, Charles Rivers, 15, 16, 17
Fort Sumter, 7, 32, 66
Foust, Benezet, 17, 18, 19
Francine, Louis, 19, 20, 21
Fredericksburg, Battle of, 12, 18, 20, 21, 29, 31, 53, 59
French, Samuel, 62, 65
Furness, Frank, 72
Gettysburg, Battle of, 1, 2, 3, 8, 13, 18, 20, 21, 24, 26, 29, 30, 31, 38, 47, 59, 65
Godey, Louis, 63, 64
Godon, Sylvanus, 21
Gregory, Edgar, 22, 23
Hale, Sarah Josepha, 63, 64
Hall, Caldwell, 23, 24
Hofmann, John, 24, 25
Kane, Thomas, 59, 65
Knowles, Oliver, 25, 26, 27
Lewis, William, 27, 28
Meade, George G., 12, 28, 29, 30, 31
Meade, George, Jr., 31, 32

Mercer, Samuel, 32, 33
Mexican War, 2, 3, 21, 28, 32, 35, 38, 40, 43, 44, 50, 51, 52, 53, 57, 62, 68
Morton, James, 33, 34
Naglee, Henry, 35, 36
Overland Campaign, 8, 26, 30, 36
Owen, Joshua, 36, 37
Painter, William, 37, 38
Patterson, Francis, 5, 23, 38, 39, 41, 42, 45, 55
Patterson, Robert, 39, 40, 41
Patterson, Robert E., 39, 41, 42
Pemberton, John, 42, 43, 44
Pendergrast, Garrett, 44, 45
Petersburg, Virginia, 5, 8, 26, 30, 34
Philadelphia Navy Yard, 11, 14, 44, 45, 57
Pitman, George, 73
Prevost, Charles, 45, 46
Price, William, 46, 47, 48
Read, George, 48, 49
Read, Thomas, 66, 67
Reilly, William, 68
Roberts, Joseph, 49, 50
Rush, Richard, 50, 51
Smith, Charles, 51, 52, 53
Storey, John, 74
Sully, Alfred, 53, 54
Thompson, Robert, 54, 55
Townsend, George, 69, 70
Tyndale, Hector, 55, 56, 57, 67
U. S. Military Academy, 6, 7, 28, 31, 33, 35, 41, 42, 49, 50, 51, 53, 55, 62
Vaughn, Pinkerton, 75
Washington Navy Yard, 11, 12, 13
Wells, Clark, 57, 58
Wilderness, Battle of The, 1, 5, 8
Wister, Langhorne, 58, 59

87

Key to Map

1. Henry Harrison Bingham
2. George A. H. Blake
3. William H. C. Bohlen
4. Gideon Clark
5. Robert Telford Clifford
6. Thomas Jefferson Cram
7. Samuel Wylie Crawford
8. Alexander Cummings
9. John A. B. Dahlgren
10. Ulric Dahlgren
11. Henry Deringer, Jr.
12. Percival Drayton
13. Charles Ellet, Jr.
14. Charles Rivers Ellet
15. Benezet Forst Foust
16. Louis Raymond Francine
17. Samuel Gibbs French
18. Frank Furness
19. Louis Antonie Godey
20. Sylvanus William Godon
21. Edgar Mantlebert Gregory
22. Sarah Josepha Buell Hale
23. Caldwell Kepple Hall
24. John William Hofmann
25. Thomas Leiper Kane
26. Oliver Blachly Knowles
27. William David Lewis, Jr.
28. George Gordon Meade
29. George Gordon Meade, Jr.
30. Samuel Mercer
31. James St. Clair Morton
32. Henry Morris Naglee
33. Joshua Thomas Owen
34. William Painter
35. Francis Engle Patterson
36. Robert Patterson
37. Robert Emmet Patterson
38. John Clifford Pemberton
39. Garrett J. Pendergrast
40. George J. Pitman
41. Charles Mallet Prevost
42. William Redwood Price
43. George Campbell Read
44. Thomas Buchanan Read
45. William Moffet Reilly
46. Joseph Roberts
47. Richard Henry Rush
48. Charles Ferguson Smith
49. John H. R. Storey
50. Alfred Sully
51. Robert Thompson
52. George Alfred Townsend
53. Hector Tyndale
54. Pinkerton Vaughn
55. Clark Henry Wells
56. Langhorne Wister